Proceedings of the 15th World Sanskrit Conference

General Editor
Radhavallabh Tripathi

Vol. III
Special Panel on Nāṭyaśāstra
Nāṭyaśāstra in the Modern World

Nāṭyaśāstra in the Modern World

Edited by
Radhavallabh Tripathi

Rashtriya Sanskrit Sansthan
Deemed University
Under M/o Human Resource Development
Govt. of India, New Delhi

PRINTWORLD
Publishers of Indian Traditions

Cataloging in Publication Data — DK
[Courtesy: D.K. Agencies (P) Ltd. <docinfo@dkagencies.com>]

World Sanskrit Conference (15th : 2012 : New Delhi, India)
Nāṭyaśastra in the modern world / edited by Radhavallabh Tripathi.
pages cm. – (Proceedings of the 15th World Sanskrit Conference ; vol. III)
Includes verses in Sanskrit (roman).
Cover title: Special panel on Nāṭyaśāstra : Nāṭyaśāstra in the modern world.
"First published in India in 2014" – Title page verso.
The 15th World Sanskrit Conference (WSC) was organized by Rashtriya Sanskrit Sansthan, New Delhi, in collaboration with the International Association of Sanskrit Studies (IASS) during 5-10 January 2012.
Includes bibliographical references.
ISBN 9788124607220

1. Bharata Muni. Nāṭyaśāstra – Congresses. 2. Theater – India – Congresses. 3. Sanskrit drama – History and criticism – Congresses. 4. Aesthetics, Indic – Congresses. I. Tripathi, Radhavallabh, 1949- editor. II. Rashtriya Sanskrit Sansthan, organizer, publisher. III. International Association of Sanskrit Studies, organizer. IV. Title. V. Title: Special panel on Nāṭyaśāstra : Nāṭyaśāstra in the modern world. VI. Series: Proceedings of the 15th World Sanskrit Conference ; vol. III.

LCC PK2931.B44W67 2012 | DDC 891.22 23

ISBN 13: 978-81-246-0722-0 ISBN 10: 81-246-0722-2
First published in India in 2014
Second impression published in 2022

Published by:
RASHTRIYA SANSKRIT SANSTHAN
56-57, Institutional Area, Janakpuri, New Delhi 110058
Phones: (011) 2852 4993, 2852 1994, 2852 4995
e-mail: rsks@nda.vsnl.net.in
Website: www.sanskrit.nic.in

and

D.K. PRINTWORLD (P) LTD.
Regd. Office: "Vedaśrī", F-395, Sudarshan Park
(Metro Station: ESI Hospital), New Delhi 110015
Phones: (011) 25453975; 25466019
e-mail: indology@dkprintworld.com
Website: www.dkprintworld.com

Printed by: D.K. Printworld (P) Ltd, New Delhi

Foreword

THE 15th World Sanskrit Conference (WSC) was organized by Rashtriya Sanskrit Sansthan, New Delhi, in collaboration with the International Association of Sanskrit Studies (IASS) during 5-10 January 2012. The Conference was conducted through twenty sections including Veda; Linguistics; Epics and Purāṇas; Tantra and Āgamas; Vyākaraṇa; Poetry, Drama and Aesthetics; Sanskrit and Asian Languages and Literatures; Sanskrit and Science; Buddhist Studies; Jain Studies; Philosophies; Religious Studies; Ritual Studies; Epigraphy; Sanskrit in Technological World; Modern Sanskrit Literature; Law and Society; and Manuscriptology along with Paṇḍitapariṣad and Kavisamavāya. Apart from these sections, the event was marked with some panels on specific themes, viz. Models and Theories in Sanskrit Grammar and Linguistics; Electronic Concordance of the Great Epics; Re-interpreting Pāṇini; New Perspectives on Scientific Literature in Sanskrit; Boundaries of Yoga in Indian Philosophical Literature; Śaiva Philosophy; Innovations in Sanskrit Pedagogy; Manuscripts and Their Intellectual Preservation; and Sanskrit in Global Perspectives, etc.

In the glorious history of this Conference encompassing more than four decades, a special panel on Nāṭyaśāstra in Modern World (as far as my understanding goes) was added for the first time on the occasion of the 15th WSC with myself as its convener.

Discussions were carried out under this panel on various issues related to texual studies in *Nāṭyaśāstra* and the deliberations covered a wide range of topics uncovering the significance that the text has acquired in the present global scenario. The panel reviewed contemporary scenario with reference to Sanskrit theatre in regional languages of India and South-East Asia with reference to the concept of regional theatres in Nāṭyaśāstra; it also focused on the regional forms of theatre as defined in the post-Nāṭyaśāstra tradition. I am grateful to all the scholars who have enriched this panel by their presentations and also sent me the revised drafts of their papers promptly.

I express my gratitude to IASS for having authorized the Rashtriya Sanskrit Sansthan to bring out all the volumes of the proceedings of the 15th WSC. I hope that the publication of this volume will stimulate the studies on *Nāṭyaśāstra*.

Radhavallabh Tripathi

Contents

Introduction

BHARATAMUNI stands as a Vyāsa in the Indian theatric universe and like Vyāsa's *Mahābhārata*, his *Nāṭyaśāstra* (*NŚ*) has remained with us as a *saṁhitā* (compendium) with a systematic presentation of the conceptual frameworks as well as the theories and practices of theatre that had evolved during a few millenniums in India before common era (BCE). The concepts are rooted in Vedas but are also correlated to traditions of the Āgamas as well as oral traditions. *Nāṭyaśāstra* has remained an *ākaragrantha* (an authentic source book) for the whole tradition of performing and literary arts that have continued in India till today. With a pluralistic approach that has been offering scope for multiple interpretations, *Nāṭyaśāstra* also initiated a process of interplay between theory and practice and correspondences between the diverse streams of Indian theatre. In this way, *Nāṭyaśāstra* continued to be rediscovered in every age.

The Discovery of the Nāṭyaśāstra in Modern World

The discovery of *Nāṭyaśāstra* during nineteenth century has been one of the most important events in the global history of aesthetics and theatre. Amongst the modern savants of oriental learning, Sir William Jones was the first scholar to have referred to *Nāṭyaśāstra* in the preface of his edition of *Abhijñānaśākuntalam* with English translation in 1789. Thereafter, H.H. Wilson in his *Select Specimens of the Theatre of Hindus* (1826) regretted the loss of the manuscripts of *Nāṭyaśāstra*. During the later half of the nineteenth century, *Nāṭyaśāstra* attracted the attention of scholars in India and Europe and it was the beginning of a global dialogue on Bharata and his theatre. However it was Fitz Edward Hall who referred to the manuscripts of *Nāṭyaśāstra* and also included some chapters from *Nāṭyaśāstra* in his edition of *Daśarūpakam* (1865).

Around 1880, Paul Regnaud published critical editions of chapters XV and XVI, and then chapters VI and VII of *Nāṭyaśāstra* with French translation. In 1888 Grosset published a critical edition of chapter XIV of *Nāṭyaśāstra*, based on five manuscripts. The Kāvyamālā (KM) edition of *Nāṭyaśāstra*, prepared on the basis of two different copies of one manuscript came out in 1894. Grosset again published a critical edition of the first fourteen chapters of *Nāṭyaśāstra* in 1898. The first volume of *Nāṭyaśāstra* with *Abhinavabhāratī* (*Abh.*), said to have been based on forty manuscripts, came out from Vadodara in 1926 under the Gaekwar Oriental Series (GOS) with Ramakrishna Kavi as its editor. Batuk Nath Sharma and Baldev Upadhyaya published another edition of *Nāṭyaśāstra* under Kashi Sanskrit Series (KSS) in 1927. Other three volumes of Vadodara edition appeared in 1934, 1954 and 1964, respectively. Meanwhile another critical edition with English translation by M.M. Ghosh appeared from Calcutta. R.S. Nagar edited the text with *Abhinavabhāratī* on the basis of the four printed editions from Delhi.

Recently, N.P. Unni has brought out a complete edition of *Nāṭyaśāstra* with English translation and notes based on the Kerala edition by Narayan Pisharoti.

To sum up, the following editions in printed form of this text are noteworthy – (i) KM edition, (ii) KSS edition, (iii) GOS edition, (iv) Kolkata edition, (v) Delhi edition, and (vi) Kerala edition.

Besides these, R. Gnoli has done a monumental work by the way of textual studies on the *rasa*-portion of *Abhinavabhāratī*.

Ramaswami, K. Krishnamurthy, T.S. Nandi and Rajendra Nanavati have made attempts at re-editing *Nāṭyaśāstra* as edited by Ramakrishna Kavi. Ramaswami utilized copies of two old manuscripts obtained from S.K. Belvelkar. He consulted as many as fifty manuscripts and also consulted the texts of Puṇḍarīka

Viṭṭhala, Śārṅgadeva, Haripāladeva, Someśvara and others for correcting the readings of chapter IV on *karaṇa*s and *aṅgahāra*s.

The manuscripts of *Nāṭyaśāstra* or their copies were acquisitioned from Almora, Andhra, Bengal, Darbhanga, Madras, Nepal, Pune, Tamil Nadu, Trivandrum, and Ujjain. The database of the manuscripts of *Nāṭyaśāstra* as given by Kapila Vatsyayan as an appendix to her monograph on Bharata's *Nāṭyaśāstra* lists 112 manuscripts. Not all of them have been properly utilized by the learned editors of different extant editions of Bharata's text. One important manuscript, still to be unearthed and utilized, is in Rajasthan. Credit goes to Kamlesh Datta Tripathi for having acquired seven new manuscripts of *Nāṭyaśāstra* from Nepal in Bhojimol, Newārī and Devanāgarī scripts. They belong to the period from thirteenth to nineteenth century CE. Ramakrishna Kavi and K. Krisnamurthi have already utilized a manuscript from Nepal in the GOS edition of *Nāṭyaśāstra* volume IV. Anvita Sharma in her paper in the present volume has tried to examine the significance of the readings in old Newārī manuscripts of *Nāṭyaśāstra*. It is clear from the deliberations of various scholars on this issue that the textual riddles of *Nāṭyaśāstra* including the text of *Abhinavabhāratī* require further investigations.

Nāṭyaśāstra and the Modern Stage

Parallel to the onslaught of European realistic theatre in India and the emergence of Parsi theatre following it, Rabindranath Tagore in Bengal and Bharatendu Harishchandra at Kāśī made pioneer attempts at recreating, regenerating and resuscitating the spirit of Indian theatre and in doing so, they revived interest in *Nāṭyaśāstra* and established the immense potential of its system for building up a national theatre. They were followed by a number of scholars and theatre experts. As a result, some institutions like the National School of Drama at Delhi, the Kalidasa Akademi at Ujjain and Kerala Kala Mandalam could take initiatives at rediscovering Bharata in our times.

This led to a discourse on the question of continuity and change in traditional Indian forms of theatre. Kapila Vatsyayan as well as many other authors have done considerable work on interlinks between *Nāṭyaśāstra* and the regional forms of theatre.

In the tradition of *Nāṭyaśāstra*, the regional forms of dance and drama are classified as *nṛttaprabandhas*, *nṛtyas*, *deśīrūpakas*, *geyarūpakas*, *anyarūpakas*, *saṁkīrṇarūpakas* and *uparūpakas*. Certain key concepts and stylizations, borrowed directly or indirectly from *Nāṭyaśāstra*, are universally accepted in almost all the regional theatres of India. These include the preliminaries or *pūrvaraṅga*, *rasa*-oriented aesthetics, the non-linear concept of time and space, and a number of theatrical conventions like *kakṣyāvibhāga* and *bhūmikāvikalpa*.

Later authors of Nāṭyaśāstra tradition like Dhanika–Dhanañjaya, Ramacandra–Guṇacandra, Hemacandra, Śārṅgadeva, Śāradātanaya, Sāgaranandin, Jāyasenāpati, Someśvara, Sudhākalaśa, Amṛtānandayogin, Viśvanātha, Kumbha, Puṇḍarīka Viṭṭhala, Śubhaṅkara, Raghunātha, Vipradāsa and others record the growth of regional forms of theatre.

Despite the apparent discontinuity of the Nāṭyaśāstra traditions in the medieval period, the legacy of Bharata thrived in textual tradition through the enormous contributions of these authors.

In my *Aspects of Nāṭyaśāstra*[1] I have discussed the following dramatic forms referred by these latter *ācāryas* – *ullopyaka* (*ullāpyaka*), *kalpavalī*, *karṇa*, *kāvya*, *goṣṭhī*, *carcaī*, *chalita* (*chālikya*), *citrakāvya* (*rāgakāvya*), *jakkaḍī*, *ḍombī*, *toṭaka* (*troṭaka*), *daṇḍarāsaka*, *durmallikā* (*durmīlitā*), *dvipadī*, *nartanaka*, *nāṭikā*, *nāṭyarāsaka*, *pārijātaka*, *piṇḍī*, *prakaraṇī*, *prasthāna*, *prekṣaṇaka* (*preṅkhaṇa*), *preraṇī* (*peraṇī*), *bhāṇa*, *bhāṇikā*, *bhāṇī*, *bhedyaka*, *maṇikulyā*, *mallikā*, *rāmākrīḍa*, *rāsaka*, *lāsaka* *lāsikā*, *vilāsikā*, *śamyā*, *śilpaka*, *śṛṅkhalā*, *śrīgadita*, *ṣidgaka*, *saṭṭaka*, *sallāpaka* (*saṁllāpaka*), *skandhaka* and *hallīsaka*.

---

[1] Kunjunni Raja Academy of Indological Research, Aluva, Kerala, 2011.

As the only standard sourcebook text of an encyclopaedic nature, *Nāṭyaśāstra* cast an everlasting influence on the regional theatric traditions not only in India but on the theatric traditions of many other Asian countries too. Its impact can be seen in Balenese or Indonesian performing arts, in Siam or Thailand or in Noah theatre of Japan. In India, various concepts – fundamental philosophy of art – have percolated so deeply through various forms of dance and drama that despite all the geographical, social and anthropological differences, this single unique text of Bharatamuni has served the cause of sustenance of and synthesis between the diverse regional theatric traditions of India. The tenets of *Nāṭyaśāstra* in some way or other are reflected in the regional theatre forms like *bhānd pather* and *bhand* of Kashmir; *aṅkiyānāṭa, lai haroaba* and *barechaharia bhāvanā* of Assam; *maṇipurīrāsa; rāmalīlā, rāsalīlā, svāṅga, nauṭaṅkī,* etc. (north India); *māca* and *nācā* (central India); *bhavāi* (Gujarat), *harikathā* and *yakṣagāna* (Karnataka and Andhra Pradesh); and *kr̥ṣṇāṭṭam, rāmanāṭṭam, therukūttu, kathakali, vīthīnāṭakam, kūṭiyāṭṭam, bhāgavatamelā,* etc. (Kerala and Tamil Nadu).

On the other hand, the interaction between *Nāṭyaśāstra* and regional theatres of India has not been a one way affair. The regional theatric traditions might have considerably contributed to the restructuring of the text of *Nāṭyaśāstra*.

There is continuity of traditions and Sanskrit theatre registers its presence in multifarious ways through diverse regional theatric forms in India.

In fact, it is owing to the appearance of *Nāṭyaśāstra* in the modern theatric scene that the efflorescence is now breathing with immense potential. Most of the eminent theatre directors are turning towards *Nāṭyaśāstra* directly or indirectly. In the latter half of the twentieth century, Sanskrit theatre emerged as a force to reckon with and the connotation of the term "Sanskrit theatre" did not remain confined to the productions of Sanskrit plays in original or translations, it incorporated modern plays adopting concepts, techniques and structures from traditional forms or *Nāṭyaśāstra*.

Therefore, Kamleshdatta Tripathi, in his paper published here, rightly views the *Nāṭyaśāstra* not only as a perennial source for the regional theatre forms, but also as a text opening new gateways to the modern theatre as well. The knowledge of *Nāṭyaśāstra* has created a movement of the "theatre of roots". Theatre directors like Kavalam Narayana Panikkar have turned to *Nāṭyaśāstra* through regional theatre forms, whereas there are many who are looking towards *Nāṭyaśāstra* for inculcating new creativity in the performance and a better understanding of theatre.

Concepts and Philosophy

Nāṭyaśāstra was compiled to set models and standards for actors, artisans and the playwrights. The fundamental concepts and key terms like *kāvya, rasa, chanda, kāma, krīḍā* or *līlā* (play), *rūpa, pratirūpa, śilpa, anukṛti* (making once again), *gīta* (song), *gāthā* and *alaṁkāra* had emerged even much before *Nāṭyaśāstra* came to be compiled. Bharatamuni imbibed the conceptual universe of the Vedic seers to build up a comprehensive aesthetic theory. He has used the term *krīḍā* (play) to define the form and function of *nāṭya* (theatre). Theatre is also described as a *krīḍanīyaka* (a device for play) [*Nāṭyaśāstra* I.11]. This was in tune with the philosophy which views the world as a *krīḍā* (play or sport) of the Devine Being. In Śaivāgamas the Devine Being is therefore described as *Krīḍāpaṇḍita* (master of play). The concept of *kāma* in *Nāṭyaśāstra* has its roots in the hymn of *Ṛgveda*. It is in this background that *kāma* has been correlated with *puruṣārtha* – or the aspirations of a man. Bharata therefore categorizes *kāma* into three types in accordance with the three *puruṣārtha*s – *dharma* (duty), *artha* (material possessions) and *mokṣa* (liberation) embracing the psychic, empirical and spiritual levels of human life, respectively [*Nāṭyaśāstra* XXII.95-98].

The paper by Natalia Lidova in this volume has assumed an added significance in this context. Lidova relocates *vṛtti* as a central concept in the realm of Indian theatric universe. She rightly views linkages between *vṛtta, itivṛtta* and *vṛtti* not only linguistically but also semantically and understands *vṛtti* as a key category of the Nāṭyaśāstra. She has made an analysis of the historical and mythological aspects of *vṛtti* tracing its transformation at various developmental stages of the ancient Indian theatre. *Vṛtta* – the all-embracing rotation of the world – is transformed into *itivṛtta*. The cosmic order finds a limited expression on the performance arena and is ruled by the specific laws of the theatre, rather than universal laws. Tracing the divine origin of *vṛtti*s, Lidova rightly points out how the aesthetics of sublimity – the divine game – was recreated on the stage.

Origin of Nāṭya

The possibilities of Greek influence over Sanskrit theatre were first discussed by orientalists like A. Weber and E. Windisch. Weber opined that the dramas performed in the court of the Greek princes in Bactria were reproduced in Punjab and Gujarat in India and they initiated beginnings of Indian theatre (*Ind. Litteratüre Geschichte*, Berlin, 1876, p. 224 refer in De and Dasgupta, *History of Sanskrit Literature*, p. 650). Jacobi, Pischel and Schroeder criticized them and proved the weakness of their arguments (De and Dasgupta, *History of Sanskrit Literature*, p. 650). In his *History of Mimic*, Hermann Reich tried to prove that mimic came to India from Greece. Max Lindenau in 1913 discussed the relation between Bharata's *Nāṭyaśāstra* and Aristotle's *Poetics* in *Beiträge zur Altindischen Rasalehre*, Lipzig, 1913 (De and Dasgupta, *History of Sanskrit Literature*, p. 53).

Before this, Indian theatre by Lévi had been published in 1890 and Keith's well-known works on the history of Sanskrit literature and Sanskrit drama came out in 1920 and 1924, respectively. Keith examined the Indian and Greek dramatic theories. These attempts heralded a beginning of global poetics and aesthetics in modern times in the Sanskrit world.

Although the exercises to investigate upon the supposed influence of Greek traditions over Sanskrit drama proved to be futile, they indirectly provoked some researchers in India to take up studies in Bharata's poetics and dramaturgy and Aristotalian *Poetics*. The issue of interrelationship between Greek dramaturgy and *Nāṭyaśāstra* has been revisited through diverse approaches till the present decade of the twenty-first century. M.L.Varadpande in his volumes of history of Indian theatre has re-examined the question of interrelationships between the Indian and Greek traditions of theatre and aesthetics during pre-Christian era. Bharata Gupta has come out with a study of Greek drama and various existing models of ancient Greek theatres to show that the two traditions have had close interconnections. The latest important work in this field is by Klara Gönc Moačanin who has been consistently pursuing researches with reference to this problem. In her paper on "Nāṭya vs. Greek Tragedy", she reopens the question of Greek influence on Sanskrit theatre to reaffirm the divergences between the two streams. However her presumption Indian theatre appeared long after Greek influence disappeared – is debatable. It stands in contravention to the theory of the origin of *nāṭya* from Vedic *yajña*, which Kamleshdatta Tripathi in his paper has referred.

Nāṭyaśāstra and the Post-Modern Theatre

Lybe Bansat Bodoun in her paper on "Artaud's Poetics, or Nāṭyaśāstra and Post-modern Theatre" shows how symbolist theatre has unknowingly embraced some features of Bharata's theatre. Artaud's concepts of "an exact amount of assured gesture", "tested mime" as well as his idea of *spiritual clothing* [in French: *enrobement spirituel*] stand in affirmation to the concept of *sāttvikābhinaya* in *Nāṭyaśāstra*. A background for this affirmation had already been created in the work of the surrealist poet, who had taught himself Sanskrit and brought out in 1935 a translation of a passage in the first chapter of *Nāṭyaśāstra*. Artaud therefore could show how the codes and conventions become creative and meaningful for theatre, which Bodoun terms here as the "gestured metaphysics" where exaggerations are used in abundance but this abundance required utmost restraint and *sādhanā* (practice).

Sonal Nimbkar and Navjyoti Singh view dance movement is not just in external body, they are structured within. Dance therefore is both "a physical and mental phenomena" where *manas* functions as "the link between *śarīra* and *ātman*". An understanding of *manas* can be helpful to understand the grammar of dance.

Nāṭyaśāstra is not just a text, it is a tradition of theatre that has remained vibrant till today.

The present volume records divergent views with regard to *Nāṭyaśāstra*. Indian scholars of *Nāṭyaśāstra* will hardly agree with Klara Gönc Moačanin adjusting *Nāṭyaśāstra* as an "anonymous work, a palimpsest belonging to Śāstric literature with its special idiolect, layers of text, interpolations, etc."

Radhavallabh Tripathi

1

Bharata's Nāṭyaśāstra and Traditional Indian Theatre

The Issue of the Identity of Indian Theatre and the Impact of Nāṭyaśāstric Tradition on the Contemporary Theatre

Kamleshdatta Tripathi

SANSKRIT theatre has emerged to occupy the central place in contemporary theatre movement in India in recent decades. Growing interest of scholars and theatre artists in the performance of Sanskrit plays and the inspiration received by the contemporary theatre directors from traditional theatre forms are clearly discernible in many of the contemporary play-productions in India. The search for the identity of Indian theatre which started in the sixth decade of twentieth century culminated in a serious enquiry into traditional theatre forms of the country as well as classical Sanskrit theatre.

The publication of Bharata's *Nāṭyaśāstra,* complete with the *Abhinavabharātī* from Baroda in 1964, coincides with a fresh interest of theatremen and artists not only in *Nāṭyaśāstra* itself but also in *kūṭiyāṭṭam* and numerous forms of traditional folk theatre scattered throughout India.

It is interesting to note how the scholars in the end of the nineteenth century and the first half of the twentieth century were groping in darkness to understand the origin of the Indian drama and theatre. Thanks to the efforts of Maria C. Bryski[1] and F.B.J. Kuiper[2] as well as some Indian scholars, the question of the origin of Indian drama has been resolved; and now it is evident that the most plausible source of the Indian theatre is the Vedic tradition itself which has assimilated the other streams of tradition as well. It is remarkable that *Nāṭyaśāstra* offers this view in the description of the myth of the origin of Nāṭyaveda, albeit in a different garb of thought and language. Moreover, *Nāṭyaśāstra* remains not only a unique encyclopaedic compendium of ancient Indian theatre, it covers a wide range of artistic subjects such as music, dance, aesthetics, architecture, and considerably depends on disciplines as diverse as philosophy, psychology, myth, ritual, grammar, phonetics and geography.

Quite astonishingly, the later forms of traditional Indian theatre developed in different regions of the country are inspired by *Nāṭyaśāstra* although they are equally rooted into their respective regional traditions and regional texts which have been evolved under the impact of *Nāṭyaśāstra*. It would not be an exaggeration to state that the practice part of *Nāṭyaśāstra* can be understood through the commentary by Abhinavagupta entitled *Nāṭyavedavivṛtti* or *Abhinavabhāratī*, as well as the stage directions provided in Sanskrit plays and the references given in different literary sources, old commentaries on the Sanskrit plays, later texts available on dance, drama and music, and commentaries thereon and pre-medieval and medieval traditional theatre forms such as *kūṭiyāṭṭam*, *yakṣagāna*, *kathakaḷī*, *aṅkiyānāṭa*, *bhāvanā*, *rāmalīlā*, *rāsa*, *bhavāi* and so on. These forms are still vibrant. In fact, the core structure of Sanskrit drama continues to develop on two parallel lines in which its two central characters, namely *sūtradhāra* and *vidūṣaka*, are constantly evolved under various different names. *Sūtradhāra* is known as *bhāgavata* in

---

1 Maria Christopher Bryski, *Concept of Ancient Indian Theatre*, New Delhi: Munshiram Manoharlal, 1974, pp. 52-61.

2 *Varuṇa and Vidūṣaka: On the Origin of Sanskrit Drama*, Amsterdam, 1976.

some regional theatres and *vidūṣaka* appears with the same name in *kūṭiyāṭṭam* and performs the same role he used to perform earlier in Sanskrit theatre.[3] However, he has been developed in various ways assuming different names and forms such as *tamāśā, bhavāi, bhāṇḍa pather, nāca* and *māca*.

This unique aspect of the continuity of traditional theatre and its interrelatedness has been clearly perceived now in the context of the movement for the search of the identity of Indian theatre. This explains why the movement leaned heavily on *Nāṭyaśāstra* as well as all literary and śāstric sources. At the same time understanding theatre forms of Indian subcontinent on the one hand and Asian theatre forms on the other has acquired an added significance. Consequently, a few noted contemporary theatre directors have utilized their understanding of *Nāṭyaśāstra* and traditional forms of theatre very creatively and, thus, they tried to rediscover the identity of Indian theatre in general and their own idiom in particular.

A misconception prevails among the historians of Sanskrit drama that there was a decline of the dramatic and theatrical tradition of Sanskrit after the ninth century CE. According to this view, the plays written in the pre-medieval and medieval periods were simply superficial emulations of the previous writings and modelled in a mechanical way on the norms prescribed in the texts of Sanskrit dramaturgy and they lacked the freshness of the great Sanskrit playwrights like Bhāsa, Kālidāsa and others. In fact, the literary value of the pre-medieval and medieval Sanskrit plays still remains to be examined and a discerning appraisal of some of the eminent playwrights like Rājaśekhara, Kṣemīśvara, Vatsarāja, Kulaśekharavarman and few others awaits the attention of the modern scholarship.

---

[3] For the function *vidūṣaka* in *kūṭiyāṭṭam*, see G. Venu, *Production of Play in Kudiattam*, Natakaivali, Ammanur Chakyar Madhom, Irinigilakuda – 680 121, Trichur, Kerala, 1989.

A vast number of the playwrights in the aforesaid period have written these plays in keeping with the changing trends of their contemporary theatre practice. There was a marked shift in pre-medieval Indian theatrical world. New trends emerged forcefully. It is remarkable that Kulaśekharavarman in the south and Rājaśekhara in the north are responsible for the continuity and innovation in the Sanskrit drama writing and they provided a fresh stimulus by assimilating new trends prevalent in their respective regions. Kulaśekharavarman infused a new strength in the age-old *kūṭiyāṭṭam* tradition of Kerala preserved by the Cākyārs and he wrote new plays also for the same. Likewise Rājaśekhara wrote plays in Sanskrit to mark the continuity of the Sanskrit plays modelled on the norms laid down in the texts on dramaturgy, particularly *Nāṭyaśāstra* and at the same time, he wrote a Prākr̥t play, *Karpūramañjarī*, first among the Prākr̥t plays available today, which is an example of *saṭṭaka*. *Saṭṭaka* is a variety of *uparūpaka* (minor play). Vatsarāja tried his hands on some of the forgotten old forms like *samavakāra* and *ḍima* of the *rūpaka*s and infused new thematic strength in the form like *prahasana*. With Kṣemīśvara the entire concept of *nāṭaka* underwent a revolutionary change.

Nāṭyaśāstra has been a perennial inspirational and regulatory source for Sanskrit theatre from the days of Kālisāsa and other Sanskrit playwrights like Śūdraka, Viśākhadatta, Bhavabhūti, Harṣa, Bhaṭṭanārāyaṇa Bodhāyana, Mahendravikrama on one hand and a determining force for the genesis of later forms of traditional Indian theatre on the other. It is also remarkable that a number of *uparūpaka*s emerge in pre-medieval India having their roots in the tradition credited to Kohala, a pupil of Bharata. Abhinavagupta, Bhoja and Śāradātanaya offer valuable information about them. This aspect of the new development of Sanskrit theatre is bound to shed new light on the continuity and growth of the traditional Indian theatre.

Besides, *Nāṭyaśāstra* is the *magnum opus* for the practitioners of Sanskrit theatre, but it is also a source for the entire tradition of

Indian poetics, dramaturgy, music, prosody, and allied arts like painting, sculpture and architecture as well. Hence it is *ākaragrantha*, astonishing work in which all the theatrical traditions of this vast peninsula, almost all the theatrical traditions of every region of Indian subcontinent are seminally present. In fact, the fundamentals of Indian theatrical tradition as enunciated in *Nāṭyaśāstra* have been diffused in every region of this country and each one of them claims to preserve a specific dimension of the Nāṭyaśāstric tradition in their own specific way. Moreover, there is a marked interaction between the pan-Indian theatre represented by Sanskrit drama on the one hand and the respective traditional theatre forms of each region of India on the other. In fact, the practice of the Nāṭyaśāstric tradition cannot be understood properly without the deeper understanding of the continuing regional theatre traditions as well as different traditional forms of Asian theatre. The theatre traditions of China, Tibet, Korea (South are North), Japan and South-East Asia, particularly that of Bali in Indonesia had a close interaction and link with Indian theatric tradition. Balinese theatre of Indonesia is directly connected with the Nāṭyaśāstric tradition. Some of the fundamental elements enumerated in *Nāṭyaśāstra*, which at present may not be clearly discernible in Indian tradition, can be easily located in the Balinese theatre.

Among all the regional theatres of Indian traditions, the tradition of the south i.e. *kūṭiyāṭṭam* tradition of Kerala and the *yakṣagāna* of Karnataka, and the *aṅkīyānāṭa-bhāvanā* tradition of Assam mark the continuity of Sanskrit theatre. While *kūṭiyāṭṭam* continues with the tradition of the performance of Sanskrit drama with the original Sanskrit text, *aṅkīyānāṭa-bhāvanā* is marked with the continuity of the same tradition interacting with the modern languages in the north and north-eastern Indian regions and Nepal.

The rise of *aṅkīyānāṭa* in Assam, *kīrtanīyā nāṭaka* in Mithilā and *nevārī nāṭaka* in Nepal is closely related in many aspects. The language which has been a vehicle of theatrical expression in all these forms is known to be *bhāṣā* in the words of the celebrated playwright

Vidyāpati. The attempt of Śaṅkaradeva to take recourse to a dramatic language known as "Brajabulī" which appears to be a fusion of Maithili, Braja, Assamia and a few others, confuses some of the modern scholars, yet the fact remains that it was a common language with which the playwrights of all the regions of north and north-east Indian subcontinent, namely, Nepal, Mithila and Assam were not only fully conversant, they adopted also this language which was probably widely understood in all these regions and beyond. This vast area included entire Bihar, Uttar Pradesh, Madhya Pradesh, Haryana and Rajasthan, and the far remote parts of the country as Gujarat, Maharashtra and Orissa (Odisha).

Śaṅkaradeva is credited with the creation of the new form of Sanskrit theatre in keeping with the regional genius of Assamese theatre and at the same time deriving the elements from *Nāṭyaśāstra* as well as prevailing theatre forms popular in regions adjoining Assam. He tried to strengthen the dramatic movement of the region in order to suit his own mission of Vaiṣṇavite Bhāgavata tradition immersed in the devotion to Rāma and Kṛṣṇa. His interaction with *ācārya*s of *bhakti* and other religious traditions and his pilgrimage to all the important *tīrtha*s (places of pilgrimage) of north India including Orissa played an important role in evolving and innovating a theatre form which marks the continuity of Sanskrit theatre and gives rise to a unique theatre. It may be pointed out that *rāmalīlā* form evolved by Tulsīdāsa and innovations made by Haridāsa in *rāsa* are posterior to Śaṅkaradeva.

New researches in the field of the origin of the traditional temple theatre forms like *rāmalīlā*, *rāsa* and so on, and the popular theatre forms taking shape outside the temple premises, show that these forms have their origin in the *uparūpaka*s like *saṅgītaka*.[4] *Rāsa* in the case of temple theatre forms and *ḍombikā* in the case of forms which

[4] Jagadish Candra Mathura and Dasharatha Ojha, *Prācīna Bhāṣā Nāṭaka*, Delhi: National Publishing House, 1975, pp. 8-11, 49-50.

developed outside the temple premises developed from *saṅgītaka*. As a dominant temple theatre form *aṅkīyānāṭa* has its affinity with *rāsa* and *rāmalīlā*.

If we examine the structure, it becomes clear that *sūtradhāra* of Sanskrit drama is developed in temple theatre traditions and *vidūṣaka* finds its development in the so-called secular forms like *tamāśā, nauṭaṅkī* and a number of other forms. *Aṅkīyānāṭa* as the principal temple theatre form develops *sūtradhāra*, besides other elements from *Nāṭyaśāstra*, namely, *raṅga, pūrvaraṅga, praveśa, nirgama, dhruvā, sthānaka, cārī* and *maṇḍala*, etc.

The plays written by Śaṅkaradeva have preserved this structure of Sanskrit plays, and preserved and developed further the performative tradition of Sanskrit theatre in consonance with the regional language, music and lifestyle.

It is remarkable that the text retains the structure of prose dialogues invariably mingled with verse on the one hand and use of Sanskrit text with Brajabulī, on the other. The theatre technique has also preserved the use of *dhruvā*-like songs coinciding with the entry as well as exit as prescribed in *Nāṭyaśāstra*. These songs, composed in a specifically inbuilt musical structure, retain the words *dhruvā* and *pada*.

The role of *sūtradhāra* in its performative aspect, who freely intervenes and carries forward the flow of the play through his comments for the benefit of audience, is a valuable source of understanding the theatre-style as well as structure of the older Sanskrit plays. It would be gainsaid that this aspect is readily available in other forms like *yakṣagāna* of Karnataka, *bhāgavatamelā* of Tamil Nadu, *rāmalīlā* and *rāsa* of Uttar Pradesh and other similar forms also prevalent in different parts of the country even today. *Rāmavijayanāṭaka* of Śaṅkaradeva is the best example in this respect. Thus *aṅkīyānāṭa* connects the tradition with plays of Kṣemīśvara and other such Sanskrit playwrights.

Kūṭiyāṭṭam has been very often defined as the traditional presentation of classical Sanskrit drama on the Kerala stage and it has also been frequently termed as the only surviving form of the Sanskrit theatre tradition in the whole of India. In fact, it is the most authentic form of ancient Indian theatre especially when we see this powerful form of theatre in the light of the description of a Sanskrit performance of *Ratnāvali*'s fourth act given by Dāmodaragupta in his *Kuṭṭanīmatam* in ninth century CE. *Kūṭiyāṭṭam* is deeply rooted in Sanskrit theatre. However, one should not forget the subtle observation of Kapila Vatsyayan:

> Into its making went many elements, some drawn from the conventions of Sanskrit theatre, both in content and form, and others which totally regional with tribal or ritualistic roots unique to Kerala.[5]

Kūṭiyāṭṭam provides an example of a most complex process for transformation of the text into performance, a valuable and unique legacy of the Nāṭyaśāstric tradition. It is a rhythmic and stylized theatre form which has been explained etymologically by K. Ayyappa Paniker as *kūṭi* meaning together and *aṭṭam* meaning acting or dancing. Thus, he gives the meaning of *kūṭiyāttam* as "ensemble acting". Identifying this form as the most complex and sophisticated among all the forms of the traditional theatre, Paniker views it as "elaborate acting" or extended performance. He maintains that the "actors are free to go beyond the verbal text of the play as written by the playwright and bring in related episodes from other texts".

When the characters recite verses, whatever be their source, they do so in a very specialized and stylized manner. The movements of the body and the gestures of the hands are highly codified. *Netrābhinaya* (movements of the eyes and eyebrows) as well as facial expressions are endowed with a lot of significance. Make-up and costume as well as stage decor are conditioned by rigid

[5] Kapila Vatsyayan, *The Arts of Kerala Kṣetram*, Cochin, 1982, p. 24.

specifications. There are ritualistic enactments which may not have any obvious or intimate connection with the text of the play concerned. Excessive stylization may at times obscure the connection between the actor's gestures and speeches on the one hand and the body movement and vocal utterances in real life on the other. Realism on the surface is thus kept to the minimum. The emphasis is thus shifted to imagined reality. And all the stage conventions are aimed at projecting this imagined reality. In other words, *nāṭyadharmī* is allowed to subsume, though not to displace, *lokadharmī*. In the use of language too, except in the case of *vidūṣaka* who uses mostly Malayalam, *vācika* is subordinated to *āṅgika* and *sāttvika*. Malayalam prose is profusely employed by *vidūṣaka*. Female characters use Prākr̥t as given in the original text.[6]

The unique traits of Sanskrit plays may be identified as a constant presence of the cosmic time in the elements of *pūrvaraṅga* (preliminaries) in which gods are invoked and the space of theatrical performance is viewed as the replica of the three lavels of universe with *brāhmamaṇḍala* as the central point and Brahmā, Oṁkāra and Indra occupying the centre as one level, the time of the performance as the second temporal level and time reflected in the time of the dramatic text forms the third level of time. Similarly, the multiple levels of language — Sanskrit, Prākr̥t and Apabhraṁśa also make Sanskrit drama unique. Both the traits have been preserved in *kūṭiyāṭṭam* with the difference that Apabhraṁśa has been replaced by the use of Malayalam in the elaborative dialogue of a *vidūṣaka*. *Vidūṣaka* also freely moves between time of the dramatic text and the time contemporaneous to him. He takes liberty to ridicule whatever and wherever he finds to be reviewed, criticized and reformed. Thus, he relates the text to temporality contemporaneous to him.

The venue of the performance of *kūṭiyāṭṭam* is the *kūttambalam*, an auditorium forming a part of the temples in Kerala. The oldest

---

[6] *Sangeeta Natak*, nos. 111-114, special issue on *kūṭiyāṭṭam*, pp. 1-2.

available examples of *kūttambalam* may be seen in their fifteenth-sixteenth century architectural frame at historical level. Yet they retain the second-fourth-century conceptual plan enshrined in *Nāṭyaśāstra* as well as in Āgamic, Tāntric and ancient Vāstu texts. These aspects have been elaborately discussed by Govardhan Panchal and Kapila Vatsyayan in their respective works.

Kūṭiyāṭṭam has also preserved many of the elements of *pūrvaraṅga* described in *Nāṭyaśāstra*. Appu Kuttan Nair has identified those elements of *pūrvaraṅga* in *kūṭiyāṭṭam* which are still preserved and those which are not preserved or which are not relevant to the form of *kūṭiyāṭṭam*. He remarks:

> We will conclude this with a short comparison of the items in *pūrvaraṅga* of *Nāṭyaśāstra* with those of *kūṭiyāṭṭam*.
>
> 1. *Pratyāhāra* of *Nāṭyaśāstra* consists of seating instrumentalists. The instrumentalists in *kūṭiyāṭṭam* are the *mizhavu* and cymbal players. *Mizhavu* is fixed in a particular position in *kūṭapasthāna* in *kūttambalam*. The Nangiyār who marks rhythm with the cymbals sits on a white cloth spread on the right hand side of the stage.
> 2. *Avataraṇam* consists in seating the singers. The singer is the same Nangiyār who plays the cymbals.
> 3. There is no *ārambha* in *kūṭiyāṭṭam* as in *Nāṭyaśāstra*, since the so-called singer does not elaborate the song.
> 4. *Mizhavu* is not tuned and hence *āsrāvaṇā* of *Nāṭyaśāstra* is also absent in *kūṭiyāṭṭam*. The mouth of *mizhavu* is covered with a particular type of leather which is soaked in water the previous day and put over the mouth. On drying, the leather gives the required sound. There used to be a *suṣira vādya* called *kurumkuzhaḷ* something of the shape of a *shehnāi* to play rhythmic tunes rather than melodious tunes. This is not used now.
> 5. *Vaktrapāṇi* is not relevant now in *kūṭiyāṭṭam*.

6. There is no stringed instrument in *kūṭiyāṭṭam* and hence no *parighaṭṭanā*.
7. *Saṁghoṭanā* of *Nāṭyaśāstra* corresponds to *mizhavu ochchapeduttal* (the sounding of the drums) of *kūṭiyāṭṭam*.
8. *Mārgasāritam* and
9. *Āsāritam* are both absent in *kūṭiyāṭṭam*.
10. *Vardhamānakam* of *Nāṭyaśāstra* can be seen in *kriyā*s like *ceria pakkam* in *kūṭiyāṭṭam*.
11. *Utthāpanam* may have its counterpart in the propitiatory stanza, *śaṅkhakṣīravapuḥ*, etc. in *kūṭiyāṭṭam*.
12. *Parivarttanam* of *Nāṭyaśāstra* corresponds to the dance *dikpālavandanam* with the song *viśvajanādhipa*, etc.
13. *Śuṣkāvakṛṣṭā* is absent in *kūṭiyāṭṭam*.
14. *Raṅgadvāra* occurs as a part of the drama in *vidūṣaka*'s *purappad* for *vācika* and *parappadu* of *nāyaka*.
15. *Cārī*, and
16. *Mahācārī*, though they cannot be seen as such in the Śiva–Pārvatīkeśādipādam description, may change in gestures. However, there is no *tāṇḍava-lāsya* or *raudra-śṛṅgāra* differentiation.
17. *Trigata* and
18. *Prarocanā* are absent in *kūṭiyāṭṭam*.[7]

Continuity of *pūrvaraṅga* in *kūṭiyāṭṭam* and other traditional theatre forms make it extremely important for understanding the journey of Sanskrit theatre, which otherwise remained obscure to the eyes of the historians of theatre.

Āhārya or the costume and the make-up highly symbolic, rich and stylized, betrays distinct regional influences. The material utilized in *āhārya* is also drawn from the regional sources. Bharata

---

[7] *Sangeeta Natak*, **111-114**: 61-62.

also lays emphasis on this regional character of *āhārya* which may freely use the materials available in the region where this tradition of performance is evolved.

It is significant that the Nāṭyaśāstric concept of *sāmānyābhinaya* — *sāttvika, āṅgika* and *vācika* in general and *vākya, sūcā* and *aṅkura* in particular — has been preserved in *kūṭiyāṭṭam* in the elements such as *nālāvr̥tti* of *vācika* and *manodharma* which retain the spirit of *āṅgika* and *sāttvika*. These aspects of *kūṭiyāṭṭam* are especially valuable for understanding the relevant chapters of *Nāṭyaśāstra* .

It is remarkable that *kūṭiyāṭṭam* has a history of about 2,000 years. Although it has passed several points of departure from second century CE to our own time through Kulaśekharavarman and Zamorin of Calicut, yet the continuity of performance of Sanskrit plays especially those of Bhāsa, Mahendravikrama and Kulaśekhara and other playwrights is the unmistakable evidence of the strength of Sanskrit theatre.

Entire Sanskrit theatre as well as all forms of traditional theatre are identified by the *rasa* experience. *Rasa*-based nature of traditional theatre continues without interruption to this date. *Kūṭiyāṭṭam* is the most powerful example of the theatre practice, which has attained its highest peak in the delineation of *bhāva*s in the process of *rasa* evocation whether it be *nālāvr̥tti* or the presentation of the dialogical text four times in course of performance or the elaborate expansion of *āṅgika abhinaya* in order to unfold the multilayered poetic meaning of the text in keeping with *āṭṭaprakāram* and *kramadīpikā* developed for plays performed in this system. Thus, *kūṭiyāṭṭam* offers the instance of highest technique developed in course of centuries. The best parallel of this elaborative technique may be seen in the present styles of north Indian music such as Dhrupada or the ancient and medieval Indian murals and folk tradition of *paṭacitra* and the sculptures on the outer walls of temples. This dimension of traditional Indian theatre and other forms of arts may be understood in the light of the concept of *bhāvānukīrtana* occurring in *Nāṭyaśāstra* and elaborated upon in *Abhinavabhāratī*.

It is a question of the presence of the degree of *nāṭyadharmī* or the stylized and conventional mode of performance in various forms of traditional theatre evolved in different regions of India. Relative emphasis on fourfold *abhinaya* and presence of the form of music which lays emphasis on percussion of four types – drums, cymbals, wind and string-instruments – as well as the emphasis on rendering of songs and playing of drums and cymbals which may be seen as guiding principles in the distinctive evolution of the different forms spread all over India.

If *kūṭiyāṭṭam* is distinct in its use of *āṅgika, sāttvika, vācika* and *āhārya,* as well as role of the drums, *aṅkiyānāṭa-bhāvanā* is marked by the predominant place of drums like *khol*, huge cymbals, rendering of the songs through vocal and instrumental music and the emphasis on the performance aspects materialized by a team of performers, the preservation of the elements of *pūrvaraṅga* in the presentation of *dhemālī* and *gāyana-vāyana*, and the specific function given to *sūtradhāra* and preservation of the elements from *sūtradhāra* to *nāndī* in *aṅkiyānāṭa-bhāvanā* texts in their performative dimension. The distinctive use of *pusta* is also a very significant element of *aṅkiyānāṭa-bhāvanā*.

Thus, these two dominant forms of the south and the north show the course of development of Indian theatre. *Kathakaḷi, yakṣagāna, bhāgavatamelā, kuruvanjī* in the south and *rāmalīlā, rāsa, prahlādanāṭaka, jātrā* and other forms in the north and a few others offer a glimpse of the evolution of the Sanskrit theatre in different regions of the country. It is also remarkable that the Nāṭyaśāstric concept of *nāṭya-maṇḍapa* continues to be present in *nāmaghara* of Assam, as much as it is reflected in *kūttambalam* in Kerala. The guiding principle for the use of space, horizontal and vertical, continues to be preserved not only in these dominant forms but in all other forms of the south and the north in their various dimensions.

These forms have influenced our contemporary theatre to a great degree and contemporary theatre-artists all over India derived their techniques and styles from the Sanskrit as well as traditional theatre forms. Dharmavira Bharati, modern Hindi playwright, departed from the structure of modern Hindi drama inspired by the Aristotelian concept. Instead, he introduced *sūtradhāra* once again in Hindi playwriting after Bharatendu and developed the new idiom of playwriting by infusing a poetic form into it. Likewise playwrights like Chandrasekhar Kambar in Karnataka and Laxmi Narayana Lal in Hindi instilled the folk form and content in modern Indian drama writing. These are merely a few instances out of many. Thus, we have now a large number of theatre directors evolving the course of contemporary Indian theatre all over India. K.N. Panikkar in Kerala and Ratan Thiam in Manipur deserve special mention. They have not only opened a new course of evolution of Indian theatre today, but have given an answer to post-modern challenge to Indian theatre in their own specific way through their distinct, yet identical theory and practice of theatre inspired by tradition.

Post-modern Challenge

This age of "new technology" and "global market" has raised serious questions about the survival and sustenance of theatre in general and has caused deep concern for the survival of "traditional Indian theatre", so to say all traditional Indian art forms, in particular. The question of extinction of traditional art forms has attracted the attention of serious artists and thinkers all over the world. Such a concern was expressed by Eugino Barba, when he organized a festival of a few traditional forms from China, Japan, South Korea, India as well as seventeenth-century European Opera in Copenhagen around CE 2000.

The challenges posed by the post-modern culture, shaped by new technology may be approached from deeper philosophical angles.

Now art forms are no more, "representational", they are taken to be generating the experience as "presence", especially in the realm of TV and video films.

The sense of distance, spatial or temporal, has vanished, thanks to the post-modern notions of speed and communication. While remaining in one part of the world, we may share the moments occurring in another remotest part of the world. Right from the sports, games and fashion parades to the TV news presentation, it is the experience of "presence" taking place "here" and "now" in our day-to-day life. This over-powering illusion of presence, caused by the electronic media, actually not just two degrees, in fact more than two degrees, away from the reality, has blurred our vision so much that we are being drifted gradually away from all representational art forms, especially the representational theatre.

Emergence of film and video has posed another challenge to theatre, especially to the traditional Asian theatrical forms. New technology has introduced a novel mode of expression what Richard Schechner would call "restoration of behaviour". A film director treats a strip of film which can be rearranged and reconstructed independent of the causal system — social, psychological or technological that brought it into existence.[8] Thus, technology has given immense power to the modern electronic mass media to alter and to focus on the reality the way they like. This awesome power is regulating and altering the response of the viewers. Language as a means of communication, controlled by the masters of media, has exercised such a terrible pressure on the minds of masses, that the people have lost all the freedom of a receptor to review and reject the thought or the experience which is being superimposed on them.

This immense power of the electronic media has forced the theatre to withdraw from public space and caused the gradual

---

[8] Richard Schechner, *Performative Circumstances from the Avant Garde to Ramlila*, Calcutta: Seagull Books, 1983, p. 164.

disappearance of the viewers of the theatre, the dwindling number of the theatre-goers and the total transformation of the public taste.

As far as the question of "restoration of behaviour" is concerned, Schechner has noticed that a similar process may be seen in theatre. He observes that originally as a process used in a process of rehearsals to make a new process – a performance – the strips of behaviour are themselves a process, rather than things, items, "material". The strips can be of long duration as in some rituals or of short duration, as in some gestures, dance movements or *mantras*.

Here, it may be emphasized that traditional Indian forms, based on the training, do not require that type of rehearsals as are needed in modern theatre. They are, therefore, essentially elaborative processes having their base on the technique of cyclical progression. They kindle the imagination of the spectators. There is yet another difference between the electronic media and the theatre. "While electronic media" requires dependence on huge resources in order to be used, theatre is relatively free from such a dependence.

However, the new technology, which has changed the nature of the "work of art" on the one hand and has empowered "electronic media" on the other to exert immense pressure on masses, poses formidable challenge to theatre in general and to traditional Indian theatre in particular.

Post-modernism, therefore, takes recourse to declare "death of theatre" on one hand and is striving hard for the emergence of a new theatre form which may be termed as "post-modern" theatre on the other. It is declared that this age is the age of TV, video, films and post-modern theatre.

The tradition of theatre emerging from the notion of theatre as "reproduction of the reality" or "mimesis" or as a reaction to it has got its own strengths/weaknesses. Hence, modern and post-modern theatre trends have been searching the answers to the questions they have been facing for the last hundred years or so.

The theatre tradition arising from the fundamentally different notion of "retelling the *bhāva*", rather than doing or reproducing the reality, as we see in Asian theatre traditions and especially in the theatre of tradition of India – folk as well as classical, cannot be defined in terms of "mimesis". Hence, there is no question of viewing it in terms of "representation" pure and simple or the "presence" as defined by post-modern thought.

However, Indian theatre tradition may be understood in terms of "representation" and "presence" as well, but "presence" is defined in a totally different perspective. Indian philosophy of language views "reality" as "being" (*sattā*), hence, for such a tradition also, there is only one time, i.e. "present". However, this "presence" may have three dimensions – past–present, present–present and future–present. Therefore, an aesthetic view arising from such a thought is totally different from the "post-modern" one which emerges from its phenomenal and empirical presuppositions.

As far as the power of the electronic media is concerned, an answer to it is the "essential autonomy" inherent in the nature of entire Asian theatre, especially Indian traditional theatre which is fundamentally a theatre of trained actors and which relies on artists, rather than the elements external to theatre proper, hence, gives true power to artists. *Kūṭiyāṭṭam* is the most powerful, highly refined example of that tradition in the south. So is the case with *aṅkīyānāṭa-bhāvanā* in north India. Deeply rooted in the Nāṭyaśātric as well as regional tradition of theatre, *kūṭiyāṭṭam* and *aṅkīyānāṭa-bhāvanā*, so to say, all Indian and Asian traditional theatre forms offer an answer to the questions raised by some of the post-modern thinkers. Based on the idea of openness of theatre, which may reveal multi-layered poetic meanings, it is fundamentally different from the "naturalistic" and "realistic" theatre. It may be nearer to the post-modern notion of theatre, to the extent it rebels against realistic theatre.

Under the prevailing socio-political scenario, theatre will definitely play a decisive role as a critique to the unjust policies of the ruling classes and their undue pressures on democratic systems. This role can be successfully played by the traditional Indian theatre provided it is handed over to a conscious and highly creative community of theatre men and at the same time retains its roots in the masses.

Asian theatre, more creative and free, is already playing its part in the arena of global theatre in this direction, as is evident from the interaction between eminent theatre directors of the West starting from Brecht and coming down to Eugiono Barba, Richard Schechner and others.

Let us hope for a better future of theatre in India, Asia and in other parts of our contemporary world.

2

The Concept of Vṛtti in Nāṭyaśāstra

Natalia Lidova

According to *Nāṭyaśāstra*, drama should be enacted with the help of devices named *vṛtti*s. Like many other categories of the ancient Indian dramatic theory, the term *vṛtti* has no precise equivalent in the European languages. It is most often interpreted as the manner or style of performance. To all appearances, *vṛtti*s originated at a very early stage in the formation of the Nāṭyaśāstra system of categories. Oblique confirmation of this point can be found in the legend on the origin of *nāṭya* in chapter I. According to it, the new knowledge of the fifth Veda, created by Brahmā at the watershed between Kṛta and Tretā Yugas in order to improve morals and rescue the degrading world was put in *prayoga* (practice) by sage Bharata. For that he resorted to the three primary *vṛtti*s – *bhāratī*, *sāttvatī* and *ārabhaṭī* – to which later was added the fourth one – *kaiśikī*.

The category of *vṛtti* is rather little studied. Apart from V. Raghavan's major contribution, which remains valuable in many respects though written about eighty years ago (Raghavan 1932-33), the bibliography on this theme is comprised of quite a few articles (Bhattacharyya 1972: 239-42; Biswal 1993: 141-50; Byrski 2011: 113-21; Ram 1988: 77-92; Wright 1963: 92-117) and scanty chapters in general studies of the ancient Indian theatre (Byrski 1979: 45-60;

Gupta 1987: 287-317; Mehta 1999: 109-28). The modest number of publications does not mean that the category of *vṛtti* is marginal or of small importance. On the contrary, it is the key category of *Nāṭyaśāstra*, as almost all its scholars pointed out (Byrski, for one, consider *vṛtti*s to be "more fundamental categories than *rūpaka*s" 1979: 45). Still the existing studies do not exhaust the topic entirely, nor do they fully explain the place of *vṛtti*s in the theoretical system of *Nāṭyaśāstra* and their interrelation with other categories. All this makes it necessary to return to the theme and analyse *vṛtti*s not only theoretically but also in the historical and mythological aspect so as to trace the transformation of the category at the various developmental stages of the ancient Indian theatre.

Let us begin with an interpretation of the term. *Vṛtti* derives from the Sanskrit root *vṛt-*, which according to Sanskrit dictionaries has the following meanings: "to turn, turn round, revolve, roll, to move or go on, proceed (in a particular way or manner), take place, occur, be performed, live, exist, remain, stay, dwell", and also "to act in any way or deal with, follow a course of conduct" and so on (Monier-Williams 1960: 1009-10). The terms *itivṛtta* and *vṛtta* also derive from the same root. Each describes an essential aspect of the object and process of imitation. The meanings "conduct" and "event" of the term *vṛtta* designate human action that the drama is called upon to imitate. Hence, the term concerns a reality more general than the scenic reality. It is the keyword in the essential definition of the drama, given by Brahmā in the treatise:

loka-vṛtta-anukaraṇaṁ nāṭyam-etan-mayā kṛtam ।
— *NŚ* I.111[1]

The imitation of the rotation of the world is *nāṭya* made by me.

[1] The majority of the quotations are from Calcutta edition of *Nāṭyaśāstra* [*Nāṭyaśāstra* 1967, 1956]. Several citations and variant readings are taken from the Baroda edition [*Nāṭyaśāstra* 1926; 1934; 1954; 1964] (GOS).

When re-created on the stage, the same events found a new quality to make the basis of the plot or scenario that *Nāṭyaśāstra* describes as *itivṛtta*. Unlike *vṛtta* – the all-embracing rotation of the world, in a way vortex-type motion, the events or actions chosen for stage performance represented minor rotation, or *itivṛtta*, confined to the conventionalized stage world and ruled by the specific laws of the theatre, rather than universal laws. Thus, the term *vṛtta* stood for real events that could be represented on the stage, and *itivṛtta* referred to the plot being enacted, while *vṛtti* characterized the basic features of the scenic action and determined the choice of practical acting devices. So *vṛtta, itivṛtta* and *vṛtti* were interlinked not only linguistically but also semantically. The category of *vṛtti* was certainly the central of all. According to *Nāṭyaśāstra*, it was far more important not only than the chosen object of imitation (*vṛtta*) but also than the plot based on it (*itivṛtta*). In other words, *the manner of action* was considered to be more significant by the ancient Indian theory of drama, than *what to enact* and *on what it should base*. This alone allows one to assume that the ancient Indian theory of the theatre aimed at its inception not to analyse the literary text of the drama, which appeared much later, but to describe the scenic action proper, which was a far more changeable reality.

This is an essential assumption, which presupposes a different view of the theatric system fixed in *Nāṭyaśāstra* and allows not only its traditional analysis as the theory of drama, but also an analysis of its own, unique aspect as the theory of the stage performance or, even more extensively, the theory of play or spectacle. The emergence of this theory directly followed from the long pre-literary developmental stage of the ancient Indian theatre. To all appearances, stage spectacles for centuries were the only form in which the drama existed. To describe such plays, ancient Indian theoreticians had to introduce a number of unconventional categories, redundant from the point of the European drama theory.

The category of *vṛtti* held pride of place among them. The author of *Nāṭyaśāstra* was fully aware of its essential character. It was not for nothing that he described *vṛtti*s as the mothers (*mātṛkā*) of *kāvya* and prefaced the description of the ten *rūpaka*s with the following definition:

> *sarveṣām-eva kāvyānāṁ mātṛkā vṛttayaḥ smṛtāḥ* ।
> — *NŚ* XX.4

> *Vṛtti*s are known as the mothers of all [kinds of] poetic works.

*Vṛtti*s had a bearing not only on the performance but also on the formal structure of plays because they were regarded as "the basis of the poetic work" (*kāvya-bandha-aśraya*). The author of *Nāṭyaśāstra* explained:

> *jātibhiḥ śrutibhiś-caiva svarā grāmatvam-āgatāḥ* ।
> *yathā tathā vṛtti-bhedaiḥ kāvya-bandhā bhavanti hi* ।।
> — *NŚ* XX.5

> As musical notes follow [a particular order] to make the scale with the basic [melodic combinations] and sounds, so the structures of poetic works emerge through division into styles.

Thus, according to *Nāṭyaśāstra*, the drama composition emerged from *vṛtti*s just as the musical scale from the notes. The subtle analogy between *vṛtti* and the note allows to discern something of pivotal importance for the understanding of the category being analysed. First, it follows that *vṛtti*s are as basic and essential to *nāṭya* as notation to music. Second, as the note is the basic component of the musical idiom and characterizes not only the sound but also the devices or recording and reading music, so *vṛtti*s reflect the essential features not only of the stage performance but also of the formal structure of the drama, while its comprehensive perception is possible during performance – which is also the case with music.

The analogy of *vṛtti*s and musical notation also helps to see why the author of the treatise chosed this category as the principal constituent and a characteristic shared by all the ten kinds of drama he described. *Nāṭyaśāstra* formulates the latter idea with the utmost clarity:

ābhyo viniḥsṛtaṁ hy etad-daśa-rūpaṁ prayogataḥ ।
— *NŚ* XX.4

The ten kinds [of drama, differing] according to [the method] of performance [on stage], emerged from them [*vṛtti*s].

The system of ideas of the drama as stage performance or play remained important even when the system of the ten ancient Indian canonical genres acquired its final shape. It was too fundamental to be undermined by another new kind of plot codifying, which had by that time emerged not only as a scenario or scenic spectacle but also as a literary text. All the ten *rūpaka*s were characterized as before on the basis of the same scheme, which formally equalized the Sanskrit literary drama and the archaic mystery genres. They had only one difference: the two best developed genres – *nāṭaka* and *prakaraṇa*, which definitely existed in the literary form – used all *vṛtti*s in their structure. Follow the imagery of musical idiom, the author of *Nāṭyaśāstra* compared them to basic scales:

grāmau pūrṇa-svarāu dvau tu yathā vai ṣaḍja madhyamau ।
sarva-vṛtti-viniṣpannau kāvya-bandhau tathā tv-imau ॥
— *NŚ* XX.6

As the two [basic] scales – *ṣaḍja* and *madhyama* – include all sounds, [only] two structures of poetic works [namely, *nāṭaka* and *prakaraṇa*] are born of all [the four] styles.

These four styles, mentioned in the myth of the opening chapter of *Nāṭyaśāstra* and named *bhāratī, sāttvatī, ārabhaṭī* and *kaiśikī* are treated in chapter XXII, titled Vṛttikalpādhyāya. *Ārabhaṭī vṛtti* represented tough masculine action based on powerful movements and gestures befitting battle scenes. Counterpoised to it was *kaiśikī vṛtti* with its feminine refinement. It based on a wide range of graceful gestures and flowing dance movements. *Sāttvatī vṛtti*, also considered of importance, was a specific style supposing that, to feel the essence and atmosphere of his part, the performer was to accumulate his spiritual energy and, in a way, turn into his hero. This style gave authenticity to acting and allowed actors to portray imitated psychological states as their own personal ones. Last but not least, *bhāratī vṛtti* characterized expressive dramatic speech.

Unlike *nāṭaka* and *prakaraṇa*, the other eight kinds of drama — *bhāṇa, samavakāra, vīthi, īhāmṛga, aṅka, vyāyoga, ḍima* and *prahasana* — did not use the graceful style or *kaiśikī vṛtti* (*NŚ* XX.8-9). The four oldest kinds of *rūpaka*s (*samavakāra, ḍima, īhāmṛga* and *vyāyoga*), which went down to the time of mystery plays and enacted battle scenes between *deva*s, *dānava*s and *rākṣasa*s, and belonged to the energetic (*āviddha*) type (*NŚ* XIV.56-58), did not include the verbal style or *bhāratī vṛtti*, either. To all appearances, they were pantomimes, bearing out the assumption of a long pre-literary developmental stage of the ancient Indian theatre.

These earlier *rūpaka*s, inclined to the battle genre, had lost a large part of their topicality by the time when *Nāṭyaśāstra* had taken its final shape, and were perceived as rather archaic. At any rate, the treatise reflects doubts and echoes debates of days long past: "These dramas, devoid of the graceful style, should be allowed [to be staged]".

kaiśikī-vṛtti-hīnāni rūpāṇy-etāni kārayet ।
— *NŚ* XX.9

The new imagery and function of the drama had an impact on the stances of medieval theoreticians, who did not fully realize the primal essence and role of the styles (Raghavan 1932-33; Bhattacharyya 1972: 239-42). Proceeding from the stage practice of their time, a majority of these theoreticians regarded *vṛtti*s as mere manners of acting, which were necessarily present in each of the ten canonical genres of the Sanskrit drama in varying combinations.

Abhinavagupta took a somewhat different stance as he pointed out the divine origin of styles. According to him, they could be made by none other than a deity with the knowledge of the transcendental pleasure or pure happiness (*ānanda*) given by the drama. He considered that the four styles had formerly had a far greater impact on the earthly world. This impact streamed down powerfully to blend with the biddings and desires of responsive human hearts and help the drama to achieve its true and sublime goals (GOS, Chap. 20, p. 85).

In this, Abhinavagupta followed *Nāṭyaśāstra*, which also mentions the divine origin of the four styles. According to the legend in chapter XXII, *vṛtti*s emerged long before *nāṭya*. In times immemorial, none other than Brahmā, the Supreme God, established *vṛtti*s in four Vedas as the universal pillars of being and the basic divine activities. At the time of another creation, when the universe was reborn after a long period of non-existence (*mahāpralaya*), Viṣṇu, in Brahmā's presence and with his assistance, re-created them anew.

This was how it happened.

> When Viṣṇu reclined on his bed of snake after making the world, [which consisted] of ocean alone, compressing the worlds with his creative power, two *asura*s, quarrelsome and intoxicated with potency, came down on him with threats.
>
> — *NŚ* XXII.2-3

As they kicked and punched Viṣṇu and insulted his ear with expletive speech, the demons shook the ocean and disturbed Brahmā, who told Viṣṇu to kill the troublemakers immediately. Then, "with refined gestures and dancing attitudes, [Viṣṇu] fought the two belligerent *daitya*s".

śuddhair-avikṛtair-aṅgaiḥ sāṅgahārais-tathā bhṛśam ।
yodhāyam-āsa tau-daityau ।। — *NŚ* XXII.10

The four primal styles created by Brahmā were used in the battle. *Bhāratī* appeared the first, when "earth was overburdened with Hari (Viṣṇu) standing on it and stomping his feet".

bhūmi-saṁsthānaiḥ saṁyoga pada-nyāsair-tadā-hares ।
atibhāro 'bhavad bhūmer ।। — *NŚ* XXII.11

Sāttvatī vṛtti appeared with the "strong, radiant, rhythmic and energetic vibrations of the [string] of [Viṣṇu's bow, named] śārṅga".

valgitaiḥ śārṅga-dhanuṣas-tīvrair-dīptikair-atha ।
sāttva-adhikair-asaṁbhrāntaiḥ ।। — *NŚ* XXII.12

When, "in diverse dancing attitudes imbued with play, the god [Viṣṇu] tied a tress of [his] hair in a loop, *kaiśikī* was created".

vicitrair-aṅgahārais-tu devo līlā-samanvitaiḥ ।
babandha yac-chikhā-paśaṁ kaiśikī tatra nirmitā ।।
— *NŚ* XXII.13

Ārabhaṭī vṛtti, made the last, "is full of wrestling positions and saturated with energy and excitement of the many kinds of steps".

saṁrambha-avega-bahulair-nānā-cārī samutthitaiḥ ।
niyuddha-karaṇaiś-citrair ।। — *NŚ* XXII.14

"Thus the [*vṛtti*s, formerly] established in the Vedas by Druhiṇa (Brahmā) with magnitude sole were re-created in the performance of the drama, enriched with *rasa*s and *bhāva*s."

tato vedeṣu nikṣipto druhiṇena māhatmanā ।
punar-nāṭya-prayoge nānā-bhāva-rasa-anvitāḥ ।।
— *NŚ* XXII.20

And then once "again on the order of Druhiṇa (Brahmā) [these *vṛtti*s consisting] of various steps were introduced by me [Viṣṇu], the archer, to [create] the rite of the drama".

punar-iṣvastra-jātena nānā-cārī-samākule ।
mayā kāvya-kriyā-hetoḥ prakṣiptā druhiṇa-ajñayā ।।
— *NŚ* XXII.23

As evidently follows from the legend, the concept of *vṛtti* was initially used to designate the various kinds of divine activity aiming to awaken universal creative powers as an earnest of another cycle of creation. The battle fought with their help also had a cosmogonist meaning because the universe again became real from a potential one through that battle.

The legend combines the various planes of being in an extremely interesting way. On the one hand, it concerns the creation of a new world in the contention between the *deva*s and the *asura*s, the two principal powers in ancient Indian cosmogony. On the other hand, it relates the origin of *nāṭya*. It includes the same four *vṛtti*s, each implementing particular forms and characteristics of the new being. Two events — the creation of the world and of the drama — are not merely combined but also imposed on each other. Thus, creation is embodied in the game while the game, with its unique laws and rules, embodies the world made.

The legend of the origin of *vṛtti*s is, in fact, yet another myth on the origin of *nāṭya*. As it told about the birth of the world and the drama, this myth might be itself a *nāṭya* enacted on the stage. Many characteristics made it extremely suitable for the plot of an early mystery drama, which, according to the legend in chapter I of *Nāṭyaśāstra*, was nothing but a battle between *deva*s and *asura*s.

As for the earthly *vṛtti*s used by Bharata to stage the world's first drama, they had to be created anew for a third time by wise brahmins on the base of the scenic idioms, gestures and other devices known as *abhinaya*s. According to *Nāṭyaśāstra* (XXII.22),

ṛṣibhis-tād-ṛśī vṛttiḥ kṛta pāṭhya-adi-saṁbhavā ।
nāṭyaveda-samutpannā vāg-aṅga-abhinaya-atmikā ।।

> [These] *vṛtti*s, made by the wise men, which took their origin in recitation and other similar things [and] emerged from the Nāṭyaveda, [had] the nature of speech, gestures and [other] means of scenic representation.

Apart from enacting the drama, they had another mission, namely worship of the gods, because

> *caritair-tasya devasya dravyaṁ yad yādṛśaṁ kṛtam* ।
> — *NŚ* XXII.21

> [The *vṛtti*s] were made by practitioners [as the] offering for the [worship] of a particular god.

Thus, though these *vṛttis* had an earthly basis and were made by *ṛṣi*s, they also had a sacral nature and served for worship.

Evidently, Nāṭyaśāstra tradition applied one term to two different phenomena. It could refer to *vṛtti*s designating the many kinds of divine activity that awakened creative universal powers in earnest of another cycle of creation. These *vṛtti*s could be used solely in the divine game equal to creation itself — a game that was the subtlest and the most interesting part of the mythologem of the four *yuga*s.

As for *vṛtti*s used since Bharata's time to enact *nāṭya*, they merely imitated the former on the principle on which this-worldly forms of play could imitate the divine game. These earthly *vṛtti*s took source in sacral texts, mainly Nāṭyaveda, which was considered the fifth Veda, created by Brahmā himself. However, *Nāṭyaśāstra* includes another statement, according to which *vṛtti*s were taken not from the fifth, theatrical, Veda but from the four preceding Vedas:

> *ṛgvedād bhāratī vṛttir yajurvedāt-tu sāttvatī* ।
> *kaiśikī sāmavedācca śeṣā cātharvaṇāt-tathā* ।।
> — *NŚ* XXII.24

Bhāratī vṛtti came from *Ṛgveda*, *sāttvatī* from *Yajurveda*, *kaiśikī*

> from *Sāmaveda*, and the remaining one (*ārabhaṭī*) from *Atharvaveda*.

Scholars frequently regard the latter testimony as yet another version of the origin of *vṛtti*s. As things really are, it is a mere specification because, when Brahmā was making Nāṭyaveda, he also

> combined the components of the four Vedas taking recitation from *Ṛgveda*, singing from *Sāmaveda*, *abhinaya*s from *Yajurveda* and *rasa*s from *Ātharvaveda*. Connected with the Vedas and the supplementary Vedas, Nāṭyaveda [was] thus made by the good Lord Brahmā, the master of all Vedas. — *NŚ* I.16-18

Thus, as they copied the divine *vṛtti*s, *ṛṣi*s had every reason to refer not only to the fifth Veda, which generalized on all the others, but also to the four previous ones, which lay at its basis, and borrow parts essential for each style from them.

As follows from the above, the original mission of *vṛtti*s made them not mere means of scenic representation and not manners of acting but kinds of sacral activities imitating divine activity that accompanied every new act of creation. Through them, earthly performances were not only analogous of the divine game but also sublime rites supporting the pillars of the degrading universe. This explains why the authors of the treatise insisted on an extremely elevated status of *nāṭya*, and regarded religious lore connected with it as yet another, fifth Veda.

Possibly, this original sacral concept of *vṛtti* survived fairly long – at any rate, while *nāṭya* remained within the ritual context and was regarded as mystery play on the renovation of the world. Much changed in the original concept of *Nāṭyaśāstra* when this premise was forgotten and the theatre accordingly lost its sacral message. In particular, it became vague why the authors of the treatise attached such tremendous importance to *vṛtti* category. The later literary dramas no longer aspired to interact with the secret universal laws. They aimed to catch human not divine attention. That was how the concept of *vṛtti* also changed to lose its link with the sublime ritual of rejuvenating the world, and adapted to the simpler needs of the literary court theatre.

A deliberate and principled shift of the initial levels of the sacral hierarchy was one of the consequences. As a result, the idea of the four *vṛtti*s as the means of creation was lost almost totally. From then on, they were perceived as analogous to *abhinaya*s — the ways of scenic representation and sets of performing techniques, which as was mentioned above the wise brahmins used to create the earthly *vṛtti*s.

The *abhinaya*s proper belonged to the pivotal categories of the ancient Indian theory of the drama, and were introduced at its earliest formative stages. Detailed description of their classes, subclasses and varieties makes a major part of *Nāṭyaśāstra* and largely determines the structure of the treatise, which gives us ample reason to regard the knowledge presented by it as the doctrine of *abhinaya*s. A definition of the term *abhinaya* occurs at the very beginning of chapter VIII, which immediately follows the parts dedicated to the theory of *rasa*. Its traditional opening is arranged as questions asked by the wise men surrounding Bharata:

> By your grace, we have heard a consistent [story] of the origin of *bhāva*s and *rasa*s. Now we want to know which kinds of scenic representation the master should use in *nāṭya*, what the reason of *abhinaya* is, and how many of its varieties are known. O blessed, please tell us the truth about it and how we should use *abhinaya* in which the desire for success is intrinsic.
>
> — *NŚ* VIII.1-3

Bharata's answer is just as traditional:

> As wise Bharata heard the wise men's words, he resumed his speech: "O you rich in your penance, I will tell you everything

> about the four *abhinayas*. [I will start with the reason] why it is named *abhinaya* and go on to describe the four [kinds] of *abhinayas*." — *NŚ* VIII.4-5, p. 115

The subsequent definition of *abhinaya* structurally resembles the definitions of the key terms in the previous chapters, VI and VII. Extremely laconic and formally prosaic, it opens with a question:

> We may be asked why it is named *abhinaya*. It is said here that *abhi* is a prefix [expressing the direction of an action], and *nī*- the root meaning "attainment". As for the suffix *ac*, [its addition to] what has been fixed as *abhini* makes the form *abhinaya* complete. This root should be [correctly] perceived in articulation [as the definition of guidance in a particular direction]. There are *ślokas* here: The [prefix] *abhi* precedes the root *nī*- with the meaning of "guided progress" and leads the performance (*prayoga*). That is why [the category thus created] is known as *abhinaya*. It is known as *abhinaya* because it discloses the various meanings of the performance and possesses varieties, supplements and complements.[2]

These definitions reveal the exceptional importance of the category that, in fact, designated the devices elaborated by the ancient Indian scenic tradition to present the plot of the drama and action ahead. Obviously, what is meant here by "drama" is not a literary work in a form fixed once and for all but scenic action proper, i.e. a far more dynamic and changeable reality, whose inimitable texture emerged before the audience's eyes. The four subtly combined *abhinayas* were the material of this texture — speech (*vācika*),

---

[2] *atrāha abhinaya iti kasmat* । *atrocyate abhīty-upasargaḥ ṇīñ iti prāpaṇārthako dhātuḥ* । *asyābhinītyevaṁ vyavasthitasya acpraty-atyayān-tasyābhinaya ity rūpaṁ siddham* । *etac-ca dhātvārthānuvacanenāvadhāryaṁ bhavati* । *atra ślokaḥ abhi-pūrvas-tu ṇīñ dhātur-ābhimukhyārtha-nirṇaye* । *yasmāt-prayogaṁ nayati tasmādabhinayaḥ smṛtaḥ* ।। *vibhāvayati yasmāc-ca nānārthān hi prayogataḥ* । *śākhāṅgopāṅga-saṁyuktas-tasmādabhinayaḥ smṛtaḥ*

— *NŚ*, p. 115; VIII.6-7

movement (*āṅgika*), the decorative (*āhārya*), comprising costumes, props and make-up and *sāttvika*, presenting manifestations of the human nature. Bharata says it explicitly:

caturvidhaś-caiva bhaven-nāṭyasyābhinayo dvijāḥ ।
aneka-bheda-bāhūlaṁ nāṭyaṁ hy-asmin pratiṣṭhitam ॥
— *NŚ* VIII.8

O ye twice born, *nāṭya* must possess four kinds of *abhinaya*. *Nāṭya* of various kinds and varieties rests on them.

The theory of *Nāṭyaśāstra* most often defined the scenic performance as *prayoga*. As was already observed, the opening chapter describes the world's first scenic production, which the sons of Bharata performed before the gods, as "*prayoga* based on the *bhāratī, sāttvatī* and *ārabhaṭī* styles" (*NŚ* I.41). Elsewhere I have analysed the meaning of the word *prayoga* in the theoretical system of *Nāṭyaśāstra* (Lidova 2007: 345-56). Ascending to the Sanskrit root √*yuj-* with the prefix *pra*, it has the basic meanings of "to yoke or join", "to unite", "to set in motion", "to practice", and "to perform" (Monier-Williams 1960: 688). The word was widely used in the ritual context, among other usages. A synonym of ritual practice, it designated the arrangement of procedures performed in a particular rite. Manuals of the ritual practice, which fixed these rules, had the same name.[3]

The application of the term to the myth performed on the stage is highly indicative. First, it comes as yet another proof of the bearers of the tradition previously regarding the drama as a ritual form related to sacrifice. Second, the word *prayoga* transfers precisely the meaning of the performance, which is expressed with no smaller precision by the words "spectacle" and "representation". In this instance, a playing area emerges, where the word "to perform" applies both to the practice of the rite and of *nāṭya* due to the scenic elements possessed by both, though to varying degrees.

---

3 For an example of the description of *prayoga* in the Vedic ritual of Cāturmāsya, see Bhide 1979: 148-63.

Thus, *abhinaya*s, which belonged to the oldest, basic layer of the theoretical concepts of *Nāṭyaśāstra*, were originally none but the means of performing the *prayoga*, thus possessing a sacral meaning of their own. This point finds oblique proof in their borrowing from *Yajurveda*, which has a closer bearing on the technical and procedural aspects of the Vedic ritual than the other Saṁhitas.

Despite that, *abhinaya*s initially occupied a far more modest place than *vr̥tti*s in the hierarchy of theoretical concepts of *Nāṭyaśāstra*. They were by no means regarded as analogous to *vr̥tti*s, differing from the latter no less than technical means differ from the desired end. It would be more precise to qualify them as components of *prayoga* and construction material of which the far more sophisticated edifices of *vr̥tti*s were built. *Vr̥tti*s, in their turn, allowed perform the *nāṭya* ritual in its integrity.

The adjustment of the theory to the radically changing practice[4] demanded a reappraisal of the ancient thesaurus of *Nāṭyaśāstra*, due to which both categories lost their original sacral content. The attempt to regard the sacral as the applied broke the initial hierarchal links to make the theory ambiguous and redundant – as was many

---

4 Though *Nāṭyaśāstra* is often regarded as a text describing the ancient Indian theatre *par excellence*, it really reflects several traditions fairly remote to each other. The oldest one was represented almost solely by scenic battles enacted by priests, which possibly included real fighting with weapons. Women took no part in performances, and female parts were performed by men. Weaponry was not used at the next stage, and the first female performers appeared, though their role remained limited and in the background for some time. Women performers made spectacular advance at the following stage, which was close to the era of the classic theatre and literary drama. This advance was directly connected with the enacted plots, which almost always rested on love affairs, with battle scenes banned. The stage of women's harem theatre can be regarded as the last. In a sense, it was diametrically opposed to the ancient *nāṭya* in terms of goals, imagery and the absence of male performers, while male parts were performed by women. All those stages – perhaps with the exception of the last one – find relevant expression in *Nāṭyaśāstra*.

times the case. To all appearances, that was what happened on the watershed when the importance of *vṛtti*s was still recognized but producers of the drama no longer oriented on them to turn to the far more explicit *abhinaya*s.

We have to acknowledge, however, that many common features of *vṛtti* and *abhinaya* are revealed by a formal, secular approach. Both categories directly pertained to the scenic action, and the number of *vṛtti*s and *abhinaya*s coincided to allow direct correlation of their varieties.

That was the simplest with *sāttvatī vṛtti* and *sāttvika abhinaya.* Both aroused *sattva* – inner spiritual energy reflected in the mythological image of the vibrant bowstring. *Sattva* is defined in the chapter on the basic kinds of *bhāva*s (emotions) preparing *rasa* as the feeling dominating the drama. Eight of them, known as the *sāttvika bhāva*s, i.e. stupor (*stambha*), perspiration (*sveda*), bristling hair (*romañca*), constricted voice (*svarasāda*), trembling (*vepathu*), change of colour (*vaivarṇya*), tears (*aśru)* and fainting (*pralaya*) (*NŚ* VII.94), base on *sattva* to greater extent than the other *bhāva*s. In this, *sattva* is understood as something "that starts in the mind and is produced by concentrated ratiocination, for *sattva* takes its origin in mental concentration"

tac-ca samāhita-manastvād-utpadyate ।
manasaḥ-samādhānāc-ca sāttva-niṣpattir-bhavati ॥
— *NŚ* VII, p. 110

Most probably, the category of *sattva* was narrowly specialized in the initial theory of *Nāṭyaśāstra*, pertaining to the unique tension of opponents standing face-to-face before battle as they summoned up courage and mobilized all their inner resources. They sought to establish contact with the universe through their mental powers (*manas*) and thus secure luck and victory. The bravado was one of the outer manifestations of this inner tension. Boasting mental and physical strength, the fighters were intimidating each other to pluck up their heart. This duel of concentrated mental powers was more than a prelude to the actual battle – it largely determined the outcome. This duel of the mind and emotion was acted out with the help of *sāttvatī vr̥tti* – a style based on the techniques of accumulating mental power, which resembled present-day oriental martial arts more than conventional scenic devices.

Actors using *sāttvika abhinaya* recurred to the same devices with one cardinal difference – the ancient technique of focusing mental powers and energy was used not to win a battle and confirm the desired model of the universe but to truly represent human reflexes. According to *Nāṭyaśāstra*,

> *romāñcāśru-vaivarṇyādiko na śakyate 'nya-manasā kartum-iti*
> *loka-svabhāvanukaraṇatvāc-ca nāṭyasya sattvam-īpsitam* ||
>
> — *NŚ* VII, p. 110

> bristling hair, tears, pallor and other [bodily manifestations] cannot be imitated unless the mind focuses on the other [creature]. Imitation of the human nature makes *sāttva* desirable in the drama.

As he concentrated on the impersonated character, the actor transformed himself, in a way. In this, *sāttvika abhinaya* created the impression of genuine feeling in the scenic representation of the eight *sāttvika bhāva*s.

We cannot rule out that its technical character made the *sāttvika abhinaya* more adaptable to the goals of the classic literary drama that *sāttvatī vr̥tti*, indissolubly connected with the ritual battle context. It was impossible to extend the field of *sattva* before its original meaning was forgotten to enable the performer accumulate mental power in the utmost concentration not for an actual victory but for the true portrayal of the vast range of human feelings and emotions.

The *ārabhaṭī vr̥tti*, used in duel scenes, probably correlated with *āṅgika abhinaya*,[5] which pertained to scenic movement and

[5] Seven chapters of the treatise, VIII to XIV, are dedicated to its description, alongside several sections on dancing. According to *Nāṭyaśāstra*, the →

gestures.[6] Though battle scenes were finally prohibited in the era of the classic theatre, the treatise retains a detailed description of movements, analogous to the martial arts side by side with graceful movements based on dancing and characteristic of the classic theatre. The *cārī*[7] movements divided in heavy and powerful (so-called "earthly" – *bhaumī*), and light and graceful, which the treatise terms "aerial" – *ākāśikī*. The earthly *cārī*s were considered fit for duel, wrestling and other such scenes (*NŚ* XI.28) while the airy ones represented archery, hurling *vajra*, fencing (*NŚ* XI.46) and the use

→ established *āṅgika abhinaya* is of three kinds: connected with the body, produced by the face, and created by movement [and] accompanied by variants, supplements and complements. And, further on:

> Concise description of [the movements] in *nāṭya* is of six parts, and divides between the [basic] and smaller parts of the body. [It] is connected with the head, arms, hips, chest, sides [and] legs. The head, arms, chest, sides, hips and legs are the six basic parts, and the eyes, brows, nose, lips, cheeks and chin, the minor parts. Producers must know the subdivisions of [this] *abhinaya* – its "branch", the dance, and the "stem". The gesture should make the branch and manifestation [of the gesture] the stem, while the dance based on the action originates from dancing movements. — *NŚ* VIII.11-15

6 Doubtless, movement played an essential part in the emergence and development of the ancient Indian theatre. No other stage tradition of the world offers such a detailed division of the various kinds of scenic movement, which determines the transposition of the characters on the stage and includes all kinds of gestures, attitudes, mime and dancing, alongside amazingly variegated mimicry involving all facial features. A unique role belonged to the hands and arms, whose movements are detailed and precise enough to be described with no exaggeration as an alphabet that bestowed semantics on the elaborate idiom of the scenic gesture. The latter point is borne out by the *Nāṭyaśāstra* itself:

> *nāsti kaścittathā 'hasto nāṭyā 'rtho 'bhinayaṁ prati* ।
> — *NŚ* IX.154

> There is no [gesture] of the hand that could not be used to express [this or that] sense of *nāṭya*.

7 *Cārī* was a movement in which all parts of the leg took part, including the foot, shin, knee and hip [*NŚ* XI.1].

of any other weapons in the battle (*cārībhiḥ śastramorṣaiś ca cāryo yuddhe ca kīrtitāḥ*) (*NŚ* XI.5). The movement representing struggle was closely connected with the various techniques of hurling missiles in the conventionalized portrayal of real martial arts and playing upon them. Sophisticated combinations of the limbs, kicks, the turns of shins, hips and the torso, scenic falls, etc. made stage fighting extremely spectacular in their vast variety.

Apart from movement, the static attitudes (*sthāna*s) also greatly contributed to the dramatic quality of the scenic battle as actors stopped in picturesque postures before hurling various missiles (*sarva śastra vimokṣaṇe*) (*NŚ* XI.50). All these attitudes or poses possessed sacral meaning and, to all appearances, were initially used to portray belligerent gods retained in traditional memory as guarding deities. The *vaiṣṇava* pose, used for discus throwing, archery, etc. associated with Viṣṇu, *samapāda* with Brahmā, *vaiśākha* with Kārttikeya, *maṇḍala* with Indra, and *ālīḍha* with Rudra (Śiva) (*NŚ* XI.51-72).

Most probably, *tāṇḍava* male dance[8] was formed in the same context. It rested on rather sophisticated dancing schemes known as *aṅgahāras*,[9] that were used in duel scenes[10] as described in the myth mentioned in *Nāṭyaśāstra* about the sacrifice of Dakṣa destroyed by Śiva.[11] The renounced and so wrathful god performs on his remains the orgiastic *tāṇḍava* dance with the help of *aṅgahāra*s.

---

8 This dance was originally added to the *pūrvaraṅga* ritual, which preceded the drama (*nānā-karaṇa-saṁyuktair aṅgahārair vibhūṣitam* || *pūrvaraṅgavidhāv asmin tvayā samyak prayujyatām*) (*NŚ* VI.13-14)

9 *nyāya-śritair aṅgahārair nyāyāc cai 'va samutthitaiḥ* (*NŚ* XI.75). Thirty-two varieties of *aṅgahāra*s find detailed description in chapter IV of the treatise (*NŚ* IV.170-245).

10 *eteṣāṁ tu pravakṣyāmi prayogaṁ karaṇāśrayam* (*NŚ* VI.28). In this instance, the reference is to so-called *karaṇa*s as parts of the ***aṅgahāra*s** (*sarveṣāmaṅgahārāṇāṁ niṣpattiḥ karaṇairyataḥ*) (*NŚ* VI.28-29).

11 *dakṣayajñe vinihate sandhyākāle maheśvaraḥ* | *aṅgahāraiḥ prānṛtyallayatālavaśānugaiaḥ* (*NŚ* VI. 256).

It leads to the destruction of the world and symbolizes the advent of the dissolution (*pralaya*).

As *Nāṭyaśāstra* testifies, *ārabhaṭī vṛtti*, with its extensive use of widely varied martial movement, stopped developing at a certain stage, just as *sāttvatī vṛtti*, remained forever connected with the imagery of the mystery battle. As for *āṅgika abhinaya*, its development continued along with *sāttvika* to enrich it with quite different gestures and movements much more topical for the classic literary theatre than battle movement, with its archaic basis. Most probably, the crucial point came with the appearance of female performers. It was conditioned by the thorough change of the general message and thematic range of the drama, aimed no longer at the change of the world by brutal male force but its transformation by required passion. The war ritual was replaced by the love rite to condition a principled change of the idiom of movement. The *lāsya* female dance, which probably emerged at the same stage, largely determined the imagery of the later Indian dancing culture.

As for the two other styles, *bhāratī* most probably correlated with the verbal component of the drama, described by *vācika abhinaya*, so that *kaiśikī vṛtti* was left alone with *āhārya abhinaya*, which prescribed the standards of scenic decoration, costume and make-up. Considering that the *kaiśikī* style was more closely connected with women than the other styles, and amply interspersed with singing, dancing and acting with graceful display of limbs, it should be much closer to *āṅgika abhinaya* – at least where the rules of female scenic movement and related graceful pantomime were concerned. The traditional memory, however, retained the link between the dance and the battle – a strong link that proved indissoluble. Battles were enacted through *ārabhaṭī vṛtti*. That was perhaps why attempts were made to connect *kaiśikī vṛtti* with another kind of expression, not pertaining to movement proper.

The link between *kaiśikī vṛtti* and *āhārya abhinaya* is quite evident in the text of *Nāṭyaśāstra*, as demonstrated by references to sumptuous attire of glowing colours, repeated in all definitions of that style. This link is alluded even in chapter I of *Nāṭyaśāstra*, which highlights exquisite attire as one of the most salient characteristics of that style (*kaiśikī ślakṣṇa-naipathyā śṛṅgāra-rasa-sambhavā*) (*NŚ* I.45). Even more explicit is the basic definition of *kaiśikī vṛtti* in chapter XXII:

yā ślakṣṇa-naipathya-viśeṣa-citrā strī-saṁyutā yā bahu-
nṛtta-gītā |
kāmopabhoga-prabhavopacārā tāṁ kaiśikīṁ vṛttim-
udāharanti ||
— *NŚ* XXII.47[12]

Whatever implies exquisite attire and varied decoration are connected with women; where there is ample singing and dancing, and conduct bred by passion, desire and pleasure, it is referred to as *kaiśikī vṛtti*.

The definition of *kaiśikī vṛtti* mentions special sumptuous raiment deliberately, as borne out by the definition of *śṛṅgāra rasa*, which is the basic emotion underlying this style. Chapter VI says that *rasa* named *śṛṅgāra*

possesses the nature of a sparkling raiment. Whatever is brilliant, pure, beautiful and glittering in the world, it is compared to *śṛṅgāra* [*rasa*]. He who wears glittering attire is referred to as [full of] *śṛṅgāra* (rejoicing). As humans are named in accordance with reliable precepts rooted in family customs, so *rasas*, *bhāvas* and [other] elements of *nāṭya* are named in accordance with reliable precepts, and their names are made according to rules. So *śṛṅgāra rasa* [is known] as made according

[12] The Baroda edition of *Nāṭyaśāstra* includes a supplementary definition that makes even greater emphasis on beautiful clothes as this style, "with its colourful attire, is connected with garlands and decorations, and the loved and much praised garments" (*citra-nepathyā* | *mālyālaṅkāra-yuktā praśasta-veṣā ca kāntā ca*, GOS XX.54).

to rules and taking its origin in sparkling raiment [chosen] by the heart.[13]

Persistent references to refined and luxurious attire in various definitions of *kaiśikī vṛtti* and description of *śṛṅgāra rasa* are hardly accidental and clearly reveal the desire to affiliate this style to *āhārya abhinaya*. However, the questions as to whether their relationship was apprehended from the very beginning or evolved during the process of partial de-sacralization of the notion of *vṛtti* remains to be answered. It is also unclear to what extent all four *vṛtti*s were associated with the context of the ritual battle, and whether the feminine style *kaiśikī* and verbal style *bhāratī* related to it as indissolubly as *sāttvatī* and *ārabhaṭī*. One of the most important evidences in favour of these connections is the legend on the origin of styles from chapter XXII of *Nāṭyaśāstra*, but the question remains whether and to what extent this myth reflects the genuine history of the concept of *vṛtti*. The further research in this direction may become essential for the clarification of these issues.

References

Bhattacharyya, S., 1972, "The Number of Vṛttis", in *Annals of Bhandarkar Oriental Research Institute*, Poona, **LIII:** 239-42.

Bhide, V.V., 1979, *The Cāturmāsya Sacrifices* (*With Special Reference to the Hiraṇyakeśi Śrautasūtra*), Pune: University of Poona.

Biswal, B., 1993, "The Concept of Vṛtti: An Analysis", in *JOIB*, **42**(I-IV): 141-50, March-June.

Byrski, M.K., 1979, *Methodology of the Analysis of Sanskrit Drama*, Warszawa: Wydawnictwa Uniwersytetu Warszawskiego.

---

[13] *ujjvala-veṣātmakaḥ* । *yatkiñcilloke śuci medhyamujjvalaṁ darśanīyaṁ vā tacchṛṅgareṇopamīyate* । *yastāvad-ujjvalaveṣaḥ sa śṛṅgāravān-ity-ucyate* । *yathā ca gotra-kulācārotpannānyāpto-padeśasiddhāni puṁsāṁ nāmāni bhavanti tathaivaiṣāṁ rasānāṁ bhāvānāṁ ca nāṭyāśritānāṁ cārthānāmācārotpannānyāptopadeśa-siddhāni nāmāni* । *evam-eṣa ācārasiddho hṛdyojjvala-veṣātmakatvācchṛṅgāro rasaḥ* (*NŚ*, pp. 84-85).

———, 2011, "The Vṛtti Theory of Communication", in *Interrelations of Indian Literature and Art*, ed. L. Sudyka, Krakôw: Ksiegarnia akademicka, pp. 113-21.

Gupta, M., 1987, *A Study of Abhinavabhāratī on Bharata's Nāṭyaśāstra and Avaloka on Dhanañjaya's Daśarūpaka* (*Dramaturgical Principles*), Delhi.

Lidova, Natalia R., 2007, "The Definition of Performance in the *Nāṭyaśāstra*", *Theatrum Mirabiliorum Indiae Orientalis, Rocznik Orientalistyczny*, **LX/2**. A volume to celebrate the 70th Birthday of Prof. Maria Krzysztof Byrski, ed. M. Nowakowska and J. Woźniak, pp. 345-56.

Mehta, T., 1999, *Sanskrit Play Production in Ancient India*, Delhi.

Monier-Williams, M., 1960, *Sanskrit-English Dictionary*, Oxford: Oxford University Press.

Nāṭyaśāstra of Bharatamuni with Commentary Abhinavabhāratī by Abhinavaguptācārya with a Preface, Appendix and Index by K.S. Ramaswami Śāstrī, vol. I, Baroda, 1926 (2nd revised edn., 1956) (GOS 36).

Nāṭyaśāstra of Bharatamuni with Commentary Abhinavabhāratī by Abhinavaguptācārya with a Preface, Appendix and Index by M. Ramakrishna Kavi, vol. II, Baroda, 1934 (GOS 68).

Nāṭyaśāstra of Bharatamuni with Commentary Abhinavabhāratī by Abhinavaguptācārya with a Preface, Appendix and Index by M. Ramakrishna Kavi, vol. III, Baroda, 1954 (GOS 124).

Nāṭyaśāstra of Bharatamuni with Commentary Abhinavabhāratī by Abhinavaguptācārya with a Preface, Appendix and Index by M. Ramakrishna Kavi and J.S. Pade, vol. IV, Baroda, 1964 (GOS 145).

Raghavan, V., 1932-33, "The Vṛttis", *Journal of Oriental Research*, Madras, 1932, **VI**(4): 346-70; Madras, 1933, **VII**(1): 33-52; 91-112.

Ram, K., 1988, "Vijñānabhikṣu's Theory of Double Reflection", *Annals of Bhandarkar Oriental Research Institute*, Poona, **LXIX**: 77-92.

The Daśarūpa or Hindu Canons of Dramaturgy by Dhanañjaya, ed. F.-E. Hall, Calcutta, Baptist Mission Pzess, 1865.

The Nāṭyaśāstra ascribed to Bharatamuni, Sanskrit Text, ed. M. Ghosh, vol. I (Chaps. I-XXVII), Calcutta, Manisha Grantholaya, 1967.

The Nāṭyaśāstra, ascribed to Bharatamuni, Sanskrit Text, ed. M. Ghosh, vol. II (Chaps. XXVIII-XXXVI), Calcutta, Hsiatic Soeiely, 1956.

Wright, J.C., 1963, "Vṛtti in the Daśarūpakavidhānādhyāya of the Abhinavabhāratī: A Study in the History of the Text of the Nāṭyaśāstra", *Bulletin of the School of Oriental and African Studies*, London, **XXVI**: 92-117.

3

Artaud's Poetics, or Nāṭyaśāstra and Post-modern Theatre*

Lyne Bansat-Boudon

Many are those who view the French poet Antonin Artaud (1896-1948) as the twentieth century's most radical influence on the Western stage. In *Le théâtre et son double* (*The Theatre and its Double*), the most famous of his writings, he attempts to redefine the nature and the purpose of drama, what the theatrical reaction of audiences should be — an experience to shake their certainty of everyday existence — and how actors should approach their work. Peter Brook (whose adaptation of the *Mahābhārata* was staged in the Théâtre des Bouffes du Nord, located in the heart of the Indian quarter of Paris), Grotowski, the Polish director,[1] the Royal Shakespeare Company, and many others have used Artaud's theories in their work, and in colleges of drama, everywhere, Artaud is obligatory reading.

The author of *The Theatre of Cruelty*[2] has met a cruel destiny. Indeed, Antonin Artaud was an exceptionally gifted man, a poet, a playwright, a draughtsman of talent, whose self-portraits are

---

* I would like to express my gratitude to Prof. Edwin Gerow who accepted to revise the English wording of this paper.

1 In Artaud's wake, Grotowski staged *Śakuntalā* (1960), aiming at ironically showing to West the stereotyped image of Eastern theater that it generally builds.

2 One of the essays of *The Theatre and its Double.*

strikingly powerful, and most of all a man of the stage. Successively associated with the symbolist Lugné-Poe, director of the Théâtre de l'Œuvre, with Charles Dullin, who had just founded the Théâtre de l'Atelier, and with Georges and Ludmilla Pitoëff, at the Comédie des Champs-Élysées, Artaud founded and directed in 1926-28 the Théâtre Alfred Jarry (after the name of the founder of the Absurd Theatre). To the activities of theatre director and playwright (his adaptation of Shelley's *The Cenci* premiered in 1935), Artaud adds those of theoretician (*The Theatre and its Double*) and of actor in theatre and movies: notably, he appeared, in 1927, as Marat in Abel Gance's "epic film", *Napoléon*, in 1928, in Carl Theodor Dreyer's *The Passion of Joan of Arc*, in the role of the monk Massieu, and, in 1935, in Gance's *Lucrèce Borgia*, as Savonarole, the vehement and doomed prophet — all "ignited" roles. Although Simone Breton describes him as an actor "beautiful as a wave, moving as a catastrophe",[3] he was also harshly criticised for the excesses of his acting, what was seen as the "suracuité de son interprétation".

Yet, in spite of so many talents, or, perhaps, because of them, Artaud suffered from nervous troubles, that is to say, from a bordering on insanity, which varied in degree and form throughout his life, taking him from asylum to asylum, till his death.

Although he associated for some time with the twentieth century's surrealist movement, he was too independent a spirit to remain linked with any school of thought. His only lasting link was with symbolist theatre (which appeared in France at the very end of the nineteenth century). In the light of my familiarity with Indian and Western aesthetics, it appears to me that symbolist theatre shares more than one feature with the aesthetics of Indian drama, although neither the theoreticians of the symbolist movement nor Artaud were aware of it. It may be noted, nevertheless, that, in their search for a genuine, archaic and ideal drama, the Symbolists included an

---

[3] Letter of Simone Breton to Denise Naville, dated 3rd October 1924, in Henri Béhar, *André Breton, le grand indésirable*, Paris: Fayard, 2005.

Indian drama in their repertory, the *Mṛcchakaṭikā*, the best-known Indian play, to Western minds, after *Śakuntalā*.[4]

In 1931, Artaud attended a performance of Balinese theatre, given in Paris at the occasion of the Colonial Exhibition. It was, for Artaud, an aesthetic shock, from which proceeded all his reflexion on theatre. In fact, his article entitled "Sur le théâtre balinais" ("On the Balinese Theatre") is the first of all the essays which Artaud will later publish under the title of *The Theatre and its Double*, his *magnum opus*, in 1938.[5]

Thus, it can be said that Balinese theatre has been the catalyst of Artaud's thinking on theatre. Artaud pays a vibrant homage to the performance:

> The first Balinese theatre presentation derives from dance, singing, mime and music — but extraordinarily little from psychological theatre such as we understand it in Europe, re-establishing theatre, from a hallucinatory and fearful angle, on a purely independent, creative level.

Even though Artaud's text, which is as much a poem as a manifesto, reiterates his condemnation of contemporary Western theatre as

---

4 On symbolist theatre, see Jacques Robichez, *Le symbolisme au théâtre. Lugné-Poe et les débuts de l'œuvre*. Paris: L'Arche, 1957.

5 Paris: Gallimard, 1938. (It contains: 1) "Le Théâtre et la peste" ("Theatre and the Plague") 1933; 2) "La Mise en scène et la métaphysique" ("Production and Metaphysics") December 1931; 3) "Le Théâtre alchimique" ("The Alchemic Theatre") 1932; 4) "Sur le théâtre balinais" ("On the Balinese Theatre") October 1931; 5) "Le Théâtre oriental et le théâtre occidental" ("Eastern and Western Theatre") between 1932 and 1935; 6) "En Finir avec les chefs-d'œuvre" ("No More Masterpieces") 1933; 7) "Théâtre et cruauté" ("Theatre and Cruelty") May 1933; 8) "Le Théâtre de la cruauté" [premier manifeste] ("The Theatre of Cruelty" [First Manifesto]) 1932; 9) "Deux Lettres sur la cruauté" ("Two letters on Cruelty"); 10) "Le Théâtre de la cruauté" [second manifeste] ("The Theatre of Cruelty" [Second Manifesto]) 1933; 11) "Un Athlétisme affectif" ("An Affective Athleticism") 1935; 12) "Le Théâtre de Séraphin" ("Seraphim's Theatre") 1936.

verbal (i.e. verbose) and psychological (what Peter Brook will later call the "deadly theatre"), yet, the emphasis is put on what had struck Artaud as corresponding to his own vision of "real" theatre: 1) the idea of a pure theatre in which staging is pre-eminent; 2) the creation of a new physical language based on "signs": the actors being no longer thought of as verbal articulators but as "spiritual signs" and "living hieroglyphs"; 3) a mental alchemy transforming a state of mind into an abstract gesture; 4) the spontaneous improvisation replaced by a mathematical precision extremely controlled and extremely ancient; 5) the requirement of extreme convention; 6) a theatre both popular and spiritual, akin to ritual; 7) the need of total theatre.

From now on, I will extensively quote Artaud, in translation — an arduous task, for his words are those of a poet endowed with a sharp vision, words unusually suited to his unprecedented vision. What strikes the reader of Artaud who is aware of Eastern theatre, whether Balinese or Indian, is the soundness of Artaud's intuitions and his deep and immediate understanding of a form that was quite new to him.

I will start with a long description in which Artaud manifests the acute sensitivity of a spectator who is also a poet:

> In fact the strange thing about all these gestures, these angular, sudden, jerky postures, these syncopated inflexions formed at the back of the throat, these musical phrases cut short, the sharded flights, rustling branches, hollow drum sounds, robot creaking, dances of animated puppets, is that: through the maze of gestures, postures, airborne cries, through their gyrations and turns, leaving not even the smallest area of stage space unused, the meaning of a new bodily language no longer based on words but on signs emerges. Those actors with their geometrical robes look like *living hieroglyphs*.[6]

[6] From now on I am emphasising Artaud's key-words or key-sentences by means of italics.

And, Artaud continues:

> These spiritual signs have an exact meaning that only strikes one intuitively, but violently enough to make any translation into logical, discursive language useless.

Here, for the first time, the seminal concept of Cruelty appears, with the adverb "violently". Cruelty, the favorite concept of Artaud, is but the "violence" inherent in true theatre, which permits us to discover the reality under, or above, reality. Thus Artaud observes in the *First Manifesto for a Theatre of Cruelty* (1932):

> No theatre is possible without an element of cruelty as its basis. In our present state of degeneration, it is through our skin that metaphysics will enter our minds.

As already alluded to in his text on the Balinese Theatre (". . . re-establishing theatre, from a hallucinatory and fearful angle . . ."), Artaud wishes to awake in the spectator a state of hallucination and fear, to "bring him face to face with an action, but without practical consequences".

Thus Artaud contrasts reality and realism: realism being condemned as the essence of Western theatre; reality, specially, a higher reality, or the highest, being celebrated as the essence of Eastern theatre. In other words, Western theatre is physical, Eastern theatre metaphysical, inasmuch as it "impos[es] on our minds something like the idea of a metaphysics coined from a new usage of gestures and speech".

I will limit myself to quoting passages in which Artaud's analysis corresponds strikingly to Indian dramatic aesthetics, which is even more remarkable inasmuch as he knew little or nothing about Indian dramatic theory — unless it was through the intermediary of his friend René Daumal. The surrealist poet, who had taught himself Sanskrit, indeed brought out in 1935 a translation of a passage in the first chapter of the *Nāṭyaśāstra*, which recounts the origin of

Indian theater.[7] Was any of this earlier discussed with Artaud? This, of course, is nothing but speculation, and it detracts not a bit from the power of Artaud's insights.

However that may be, one has the feeling, while reading *The Theatre and its double*, that the Indian universe inhabits a part of Artaud's imagination, as might indicate, for example, his notion of the actor as an "affective athlete"[8] the basis of whose performance is breath control — a notion that perhaps reflects the influence of another of Artaud's contemporaries, René Guénon.

Thus I will attempt to show how the dramatic principles that Artaud has derived from Balinese theatre correspond to the strictures of Indian dramatic theory. For instance, a statement such as: "The play does not develop through the sentiments but through states of mind, themselves ossified and reduced into gestures that are outlines" seems to echo Indian aesthetics, as applied to drama, namely the notion that *rasa*s, which are the sublimated *bhāva*s of ordinary life, are to be translated into *abhinaya*.[9]

Not only has he recognised the formal perfection of the Balinese performance, that is, the perfection of its bodily gestures and facial renderings, but he has intuitively discovered the spiritual fountain from which emerges such a notion of gesture; in Indian terms, he has discovered the *sāttvikābhinaya* underlying the *āṅgikābhinaya*.[10] Likewise, he has understood that such a refined and conventional art is the product of a tradition:

---

7 *L'origine du théâtre de Bharata*, written in 1935, published in *Bharata: L'origine du Théâtre. La Poésie et la Musique en Inde*. Paris: Gallimard, 1970.

8 See "An Affective Athletism" in *The Theatre and its double*.

9 On this process and the four registers of the *abhinaya*, see Lyne Bansat-Boudon, *Poétique du théâtre indien: Lectures du Nāṭyaśāstra*. Paris: Ecole Française d'Extrême-Orient (Publ. EFEO 169), 1992: 109-117, 145-155.

10 On the *sāttvikābhinaya*, see Lyne Bansat-Boudon, op. cit.: 148.

> One of the reasons for our delight in this *faultless* show lies precisely in the use these actors make of an exact amount of assured gesture, tried and tested mime coming in at the appointed place, and even more [and here comes the notion of *sāttvikābhinaya*] in the *spiritual clothing* [in French: "enrobement spirituel"], that is, in the deep shaded study which governs the elaboration of those mimics, of those effective signs, giving us the impression that their effectiveness has not become weakened *over the centuries*.

And, about convention, Artaud rightly observes:

> The Balinese theatre, with gestures and a variety of mime to suit all occasions in life reinstate the superior value of theatre conventions, demonstrate the effectiveness and greater active value of a certain number of well-learnt and above all masterfully applied conventions.

I should add that the description applies as well to the very elaborate system of Indian dramatic conventions (*dharmī*), as expounded in the *Nāṭyaśāstra* (thirteenth chapter). There are two orders of convention, the *nāṭyadharmī* presenting a higher degree of stylisation than the *lokadharmī*.[11]

One can marvel at such lucidity. A few hours performance is enough to understand that such a codified art, from which improvisation appears to be excluded, far from being dry and hollow repetition, becomes all the more vivid, deriving its wonderful richness and variety from stability itself. Artaud concludes:

> We get a marvellous feeling of richness, fantasy, and bounteous lavishness emanating from this show regulated with a maddeningly awareness of the details.

In the same way, Artaud has grasped the main feature of this theatre: it is total theatre, as Indian drama also is [12] — a concept

---

[11] On the two *dharmīs*, see Lyne Bansat-Boudon, op. cit.: 155-169.

[12] On Indian drama as total theatre — text and acting, associated with →

that, from now on, Artaud will make his own, and which he will try to put into practice, as well as will also his "post-modern" followers. How aptly he speaks of the correlations manifested in the Balinese presentation!:

> The most imperious correlations burst forth from sight to earing, from intellect to sensitivity, from a character's gesture to the evocation of a plant's movements through the aid of the cry of a musical instrument.

And he concludes with an encomium of Eastern theatre, which is, at the same time, a condemnation of the Western:

> Our theatre has never grasped this gestured metaphysics nor known how to make use of music for so direct, so concrete, dramatic purposes. *Our purely verbal theatre, unaware of the sum total of theatre*, that is, of everything that exists spatially, that is measured and circumscribed in space, having spatial density — I mean: movements, forms, colours, vibrations, postures, shouts — *that theatre of ours could learn a lesson in spirituality from the Balinese theatre* with regard to what is indeterminable and depends on the mind's suggestive power.

I will stop my quotations here. As I have attempted to show, the triumph of the Balinese theatre celebrated by Artaud is to from extent that of Indian theatre as well. Whatever may be the historical relation of Balinese to Indian theatre, it is indubitable that they share the same principles, conventions, and the same idea of what makes for good theatre. Conceived as total art, theatre participates in and derives from a tradition which privileges a relaxed sense of time, an extreme artificiality of convention, and reserves a crucial place for the techniques of acting.

This Balinese presentation was not the first appearance of Eastern theatre in France. Already, on the occasion of the Universal

→ song, music and dance — and the corresponding myth of origin, see Lyne Bansat-Boudon (ed.), *Théâtre de l'Inde ancienne*. Paris: Gallimard (Bibliothèque de La Pléiade), 2006: xxxiv-xxxv.

Exhibition of 1889, a troup of Javanese dancers gave performances in Paris. In 1906, Auguste Rodin, the famous sculptor, painted a Cambodian danseuse, a painting which anticipates Artaud's apt description twenty-five years later of the Balinese practice. Yet, the true meeting of Eastern and Western theatre awaited Artaud, his poetical vision and theoretical insight.

Let us recapitulate what Artaud retained from witnessing the Balinese theatre as he attempted to build his theory for renewing the Western stage. Theatre should be a theatre of exaggerated theatricality, making use of extreme convention, of stylised gestures, of masks, of shouts rather than words, a "théâtre de la démesure" (as it is formulated in French), that is, a theatre of exaggeration, which paradoxically would be regulated excess, a theatre which is nothing but the actor, which can do without everything but the actor (that is, which can do without settings, props, etc.), a theatre in which the actor signifies — "makes sign", or, in other words, makes sense.

Such was the impulsion given to Artaud's thought by the Balinese theatre. Yet, the introduction of cruelty makes Artaud's conception of theatre altogether original and distinct from the Eastern. A cruelty which is also that of his own destiny — his "insanity" — as well as that of his time and place — Europe between the wars, source of the atrocities that will follow.

Could such a high idea of theatre be put into practice in the West? Wasn't it doomed to fail, just as failed, at the turn of the nineteenth and twentieth centuries, the symbolist ideal of "pure theatre"?

Contrary to expectation, Artaud's demanding idea of theatre not only survived, but has a long and vivid posterity, mainly due to three concepts: the concept of total theatre, that of a theatre of cruelty, and that of a curative, that is, cathartic, theatre, able to disturb all routine, to reveal the true reality, to lance abscesses, as the metaphor of the plague does for Artaud (see "Theatre and the

Plague"). It is in this way that Artaud renews Aristotle's concept of *catharsis*.

In the twentieth century, a body of critical and evaluative writing has developed which examines drama in all its aspects, especially its role as a factor in human evolution and as enriching life. Shaw, Stanislavsky, Piscator, Brecht, Grotowski, Kantor, Brook, are only a few of those who have written about the theatre, but no one has been more wide-ranging and powerful as Artaud — whose work and ideas have, incidentally, much influenced the last three named. According to Artaud, the fascination of the theatre, condemned by Saint-Augustine because of its power to drive men mad, lies in its ability to change the course of events: mankind prefers to live in an illusory world of security, believing that the fabric of social living and an ordered society protect it from the terrors of the unknown. The role of theatre must be to shake us out of our complacency and delusions of security.

The phrase most often associated with Artaud is the "Theatre of Cruelty", title of a central chapter of *The Theatre and its Double*. Artaud's followers have tried to put this concept into practice. For instance, Peter Brook's "Theatre of Cruelty" season, in 1964, gave London a taste of Artaudian theatre in its most didactic form. Theatre is pure poetry, disorientating the public from the certainties of everyday existence and taking them away. Artaud's notion is that the theatre must above all concern itself with subject matter that is relevant to its time, and not only not ignore the horrors of the moment, but, if possible, portray them as even more horrible, with the aid of imagination. This means that acting styles must be extremely physical, as primitive as possible in showing the essential brutishness of man.

On the other hand, Artaud's theatre is total theatre, a concept also envisaged by Piscator, Brecht and Claudel. In France, Jean-Louis Barrault, as actor and director, brought to the stage that total theatre, although without retaining its dimension of cruelty. Peter

Brook, usually working with more limited means and a polyglot multi-ethnic company of actors, has created his own versions of total theatre, mainly by following the basic Artaudian principle of disturbing the audience's complacent certainty that it is just sitting in a theatre watching a play. Before he moved to France, there was often vociferous political objection from parts of the British public and the tabloid press, especially to his "Theatre of Cruelty" season and such plays as *Marat/Sade* and *US*, the latter an attack on the American conduct of the Vietnam war. There have also been other 'Artaudian' companies, such as Julian Beck's Living Theatre.

Artaud's theatrical ideas, when put into practice, have the effect of galvanising the audience, making it more alive and aware, sometimes politicising it, but above all bringing an element of magic into life, with pure poetry as its major component. Beckett, Ionesco and the later "Absurdist" playwrights such as Fernando Arrabal owe something to Artaud as do the directors associated with total and poetic theatre.

In a century that has known unparalleled savagery, the concept of cruelty as a means of artistic concentration should not be so alien or difficult to understand. It is not (or not just) a matter of bloodshed or sadism, crucified flesh or martyred enemies, but rather, in Artaud's words, of a "strict control and submission to necessity".

Artaud's aim was to take the theatre out of the context of mere entertainment and into that of education, or rather initiation into a higher spiritual reality.[13] It is in this sense that Jane Goodall has considered Artaud a modern Gnostic.[14]

The discovery of Eastern theatre was decisive for Artaud's theories, and Artaud retained as principles of his "Theatre of Cruelty" features which we know to be characteristic of the Balinese

---

[13] For Artaud's followers, that higher reality was mainly political.

[14] Jane Goodall, *Artaud and the Gnostic Drama*. Oxford: Clarendon Press; Oxford/New York: Oxford University Press, 1994.

theatre. Yet Artaud's theatre is cruel, in the sense that such cruelty proceeds from a tragic vision of man and the universe, a tragic vision which is altogether unknown in Asian theatre, whether Indonesian or Indian.[15] As a theorist on theatre, Artaud remains, in spite of his extreme sensitivity to other forms of thought or art, that is, to all forms of alterity, a man from West, for whom theatre is, in essence, tragedy.

To conclude, I would like to refer to an anecdote: it is said that, in Steven Spielberg's *Jurassic Park*, the computer generated pictures were animated thanks to preliminary work which consisted in spliting up gestures of the Balinese dancers on video — a story that suggests that such gestures may be considered archetypes of movement. This is another example of the ways Asian theatre goes on having an impact on our "post-modernity".

---

[15] On the absence of tragedy in Indian drama, see Lyne Bansat-Boudon (ed.), *Théâtre de l'Inde ancienne*. Paris : Gallimard (Bibliothèque de La Pléiade), 2006: xliii-xlvii and 1190-1192 (Notice on Bhāsa).

4

Nāṭya vs. Greek Tragedy

Klara Gönc Moačanin

THE influence of Greek drama over the theatrical art of *nāṭya* as argued by some researchers is still an unsolved problem, almost a mystery.

Indologists were perplexed with the newly discovered art of *nāṭya* when William Jones published his English translation of Kālidāsa's *Śakuntalā* in 1789, as it revealed a new theatrical art. When a new cultural phenomenon appears, which seems strange and is difficult to understand, the first attempt is to compare it with what is already known and familiar.

In the nineteenth century and in the first decades of the twentieth century, German Indologists, who were also classical philologists, started with theories about the connection of *nāṭya* with ancient Greek theatre. Though Greek tragedy was first mentioned as a theatrical form that made influence on the formation of *nāṭya*, it was soon realized that some other antique theatrical forms might have been closer to *nāṭya* than Greek tragedy. The analysis of the different theories about beginning of Indian theatre has been made by F.B.J. Kuiper in his book *Varuṇa and Vidūṣaka*:

> The old idea of a Greek origin and that of the Greek–Roman pantomime being the source of the (north) Indian drama have been definitively refuted.[1]

[1] Kuiper 1997: 110.

Theory of the Greek origin started with Albrecht Weber[2] and was continued by Ernst Windisch in his work about Greek influence on Indian drama (*Der griechische Einfluss im indischen Drama*).[3] Windisch mostly concentrated on the new Attic comedy[4] whose main authors were Menander[5] and Philemon[6]. His main arguments were stock characters and some stock devices as *anagnorisis* in comedy compared with *abhijñāna*. But if one carefully studies these concepts it is easy to conclude that they are completely of a different nature. As an example he gave Śūdraka's *Mṛcchakaṭikam* which in my opinion cannot be compared to new Attic comedy which was popular from last decades of fourth century BCE to middle of the third century BCE:

> The plays were divided in five acts separated by irrelevant choral interludes performed by a chorus which took no other part in the play and whose songs have not survived . . . masks were retained.[7]

That the characters were stereotyped and plots were realistic do not show that there could ever have been any connection with Śūdraka's *prakaraṇa*.

Hermann Reich's theory of Graeco–Roman pantomime as a source of *nāṭya* and the influence of Plautus and Terence, who modified new Attic comedy to suit to Latin taste, as presented in his book on mime *Der Mimus* in 1903, is nowadays abandoned.[8]

---

[2] See the reference in Kuiper 1979: 110, fn. 3.

[3] Windisch 1920: 398-405.

[4] About new Attic/Greek comedy cf. *The Oxford Companion to Classical Civilization* 2004: 189-90; *The Oxford Companion to Classical Literature* 2005: 149-50; *The Oxford Dictionary of the Classical World* 2005: 172-73. These are short references to the subject and there exists an extensive literature on the subject of Greek comedy.

[5] *The Oxford Dictionary of the Classical World* 2005: 467.

[6] Op. cit.: 559.

[7] *The Oxford Companion to Classical Literature* 2005: 149-150.

Goblet de Alviella writing about Greek influence on India thinks that maybe something similar could have happened in India.[9]

In 1913, Max Lindenau writing about contributions to *rasa* theory in his *Beiträge zur indischen Rasalehre* daringly concluded that Bharata, the mythic author of *Nāṭyaśāstra*, knew Aristotle's famous law of dramatic unities of time, place and action.[10] That is unacceptable because Aristotle lived in fourth century BCE and *Nāṭyaśāstra* is much later.[11] Besides, *Nāṭyaśāstra* is anonymous work, a palimpsest belonging to Śāstric literature with its special idiolect, layers of text, interpolations, etc.[12]

Some authors cited Plutarch mentioning that Alexander the Great (327-24 BCE in India) had with him on his war campaigns Greek artists performing tragedy.[13] If it was so, in my opinion, they could have only made recitations from the works of Greek tragedians, there was no *chorus* nor the performing place for tragedies. But no one has yet been able to prove that actors accompanied Alexander on his Indian campaign. Though there are analogies between Greek tragedy and *nāṭya*, as we shall see later, it does not prove direct Greek influence and I agree with Sylvain Lévi's view citing Pischel that to think that Greek theatre had some influence on Indian theatre shows the same ignorance of Greek theatre and of Indian theatre.[14]

---

8 Cf. Kuiper 1979: 110.

9 Goblet de Alviella 1926: 101.

10 Lindenau 1913, 1914: 38-42.

11 In my opinion the *Nāṭyaśāstra* as we have it belongs to Gupta period, see Gönc Moačanin 2002: 221-38.

12 Gönc Moačanin, Does śāstric literature use stylistic devices? — the example of the *Nāṭyaśāstra* published in *Stylistic Devices in Indian Literature and Art*, ed. G. Boccali and E. Mucciarelli, Milano, Cisalpino, 2013, pp. 97-105.

13 Keith 1970: 59.

14 Sylvain Lévi 1890: 344, fn. 3 (Pischel is unavailable to me).

Now we come to a new discovery made in 1970s by French archaeologist Paul Bernard who excavated a huge theatre in the place Aï Khanoum in Afghanistan.[15] Bernard who excavated the site where a Greek theatre with auditorium for about 6,000 persons was found, reopened the old issue of possible Western influence on Indian theatre which was raised earlier by Tarn.[16] K. Karttunen thinks that the site was an important centre of Hellenistic Bactria, probably the ancient Alexandria on the Oxus, originally founded by Alexander as a military colony, but the question seems to remain unresolved.[17] But though Karttunen states that Greeks in the East must necessarily have had Greek literature, he is cautious and says that "of Indo–Greek literature we still have no evidence at all".[18] It is my considered view that Plutarch's reference to Sophocles and Euripides being read at Gedrosia (De Alex. Virt.)[19] does not show that tragedies were performed though why such a huge theatre in Aï Khanoum (third-second century BCE) remains a mystery for me. Bernard in his article on the excavations in Aï Khanoum (1976-77) describes what had been found of the theatre – a part of the gateways to the performing area (*parodos*), dancing place for the chorus (*orchestra*) with diameter of 13 m, auditorium (*koilon*), special seats for dignitaries (*proedrie*), which all shows similarities with other Hellenistic theatres.[20]

R.A. Jairazbhoy in his book on foreign influence in ancient India is not convincing with his ideas that Bhāsa's *Svapnavāsavadattā* was based on Euripides' play *Alcestis* and that Sophocles was acted in India as at least the theme of one of his plays was known as a fragment of a vase of local manufacture found near Peshawar

[15] Bernard 1978: 421-63.

[16] Cf. K. Karttunen 1997: 278, fn. 139.

[17] K. Karttunen 1997: 278-79.

[18] Op. cit.: 285.

[19] Ibid. 1997: 285.

[20] About theatre at Aï Khanoum, see Bernard 1978: 429-41.

showing a scene from *Antigone* in which Haemon begs Creon for Antigone's life.[21]

A.B. Keith is more cautious when he says:

> We cannot assuredly deny the possibility of Greek influence, in the sense that Weber admitted the probability; the drama, or the mime, may, as played at Greek courts, have aided in the development of a true drama, but the evidence leaves only a negative answer to the search for the positive signs of influence.[22]

As to my knowledge there exists no evidence of the representation of Greek dramas at the courts of Grecian kings in Bactria, Punjab, Gujarat so far that Greek supremacy extended. The existing state of researches on this problem does not convincingly lead to any internal connection of *nāṭya* with Greek drama.

Meghasthenes, the ambassador of Seleukos Nikator at the court of Candragupta Maurya from 303–290 BCE, never mentioned any theatrical performance. Though, it has to be noted, only fragments of his book on India (*Indika*) are preserved in the works of later authors (Strabo, Diodorus Siculus, Pliny the Elder, Arrian).

The statement of Pischel suggesting that if someone borrowed from the other side, then it were Greeks that borrowed from Indians,[23] is absolutely unacceptable. Indian theatre appeared long after Greek influence disappeared. In Indian literature even the name of Alexander the Great was never mentioned.

I shall now point to some analogies in both theatrical forms. To compare Greek tragedy[24] and *nāṭya* might seem strange but both these theatrical forms belong to what Richard Wagner called

---

21 Jairazbhoy 1963: 102.

22 Keith 1970: 68.

23 Winternitz 1968: 178.

24 I think of a Greek tragedy of fifth century BCE while it was a solemn part of Dionysic festivities.

Gesamtkunstwerk. In theatrical terminology both the dramatic arts belong to the modern concept of total theatre. That means that they included text, music, dance and acting. Greek tragedy and Indian *nāṭya* are both an artistic expression of the classical period of each of the cultures they belonged to – tragedy flourished in Pericles' Athens of the fifth century BCE and *nāṭya's* flourishing was during the apogee of Gupta period (fourth-sixth centuries CE).[25]

The question of the performance is of key importance. The performing characteristics are directly connected with the structure of the dramatic text as well as the material possibilities of the performing art shaping the dramatic text.[26]

What can be compared? There are few theatrical elements that are analogous as prologue, the text, epilogue, the music and the dance, scene and stage properties as well as one might call the artistic goal – in Greek tragedy, *catharsis*, in *nāṭya*, *rasa*.

A comparison of the parts of the performance shows some interesting structural and semantic analogies: The prologue in Greek tragedy corresponds to the function of *prastāvanā* / *āmukha* in *nāṭya*. *Proagon* was a preliminary ceremony where the poets appeared before the public with their choruses. The actors, presented their introductions to the plays with which they were to compete. These presentations were given a few days before the theatrical competition started.[27] In *nāṭya*, *prastāvanā* was a part of the text of the drama.

The text was of primary importance; it was of high artistic quality and based on earlier literary works, especially on epic literature. The text of a play was designed with a structure in difference to other forms of literature mixing prose with verse.

---

25 Gönc Moačanin 1999: 245.

26 Gönc Moačanin 2002: 256.

27 It shows that *proagon* and *pūrvaraṅga* cannot be compared. About *pūrvaraṅga* see Gönc Moačanin 2006 (forthcoming) and 2011: 123-36.

The lyrical parts prevailed in *nāṭya*. One can compare *rhesis*, the prose part of tragedy, with the prose in *nāṭya*. On the other hand, *nāṭya* does not use the kind of dialogue having questions-and-answers which is the characteristic of *stichomity* in the tragedy.

The use of languages and dialects is also comparable – in tragedy Attic for dialogues, Doric and Aeolic in lyrical parts, in *nāṭya* Sanskrit and Prākṛts. All this testifies to linguistic polyphony.

The performance schedule in tragedy is different from that in *nāṭya* as it consists of three tragedies and one satyr play. *Nāṭya*'s performance consists only of a presentation of some specific *rūpaka* or one of the ten major forms of drama; of which *nāṭaka*, *prakaraṇa*, *prahasana* and *bhāṇa* were more often written and performed than other *rūpaka*s.

The role of *vidūṣaka* in *nāṭya* can be compared with the humorous elements of the satyr play which was the part of the performance of tragedy, as its schedule consisted of three tragedies and one satyr play.

A comparison of the structures of the texts might be useful, for example, the number of episodes or the position of choral odes between episodes in tragedy. It is interesting to compare those divisions with the divisions of *avasthā*s and *sandhyaṅga*s in the dramaturgy of *nāṭya*. Also valuable is the comparison of the concepts of acting, *mimesis* in Greek tragedy, *anukaraṇa/anukṛti* in *nāṭya*. *Arthopakṣepaka*s in *nāṭya*, e.g. *viṣkambhaka* and *praveśaka* might have had the same role as messenger scenes in Greek tragedy.

The text has been organized in the framework of the music and the dance which can be seen as a kind of a meta-text. The musical accompaniment and the dance choreography greatly enriched the aesthetic experience of the text. Can we compare the lyric interludes of tragedy with *lāsya* and *dhruvā* in *nāṭya*? Is it possible to compare the choral songs with *dhruvā*s? The choral song in tragedy was accompanied by dance, and *dhruvā*s in *nāṭya* were accompanied by different *karaṇa*s and *lāsya*s.

The use of instruments and monodian music are comparable. Also, the special role of drum in *nāṭya* marked with rhythm can be compared with the importance of use of different metres and scanning in Greek tragedy.

The number of performers was very different — tragedy had three actors and a chorus, *nāṭya* used many actors but without chorus. In tragedy the chorus danced, as for *nāṭya*, it is questionable whether the main actor *nāyaka* danced or only exhibited different choreographical patterns; it seems that only female dancers danced — it is not clear whether the actor in *nāṭya* danced.

The use of scene and stage properties were also analogous. The stage was never empty during a performance — in tragedy the chorus, in *nāṭya* the musicians, were present on the stage. The scenic arrangements were scarce but the role of masks in tragedy and *āhārya* in *nāṭya*, as well as the symbolism of the costumes were emphasized. The role of the masks and make-up was to define characters by type, as there were no individuals in the modern sense of the word, not even in tragedy. The mask was the sole reality; the character was the mask. In tragedy one actor could play few roles and few actors could have performed one role behind the masks but in *nāṭya* characters are all fixed and do not change.

A comparative analysis of tragedy and *nāṭya* could help us in understanding their aesthetic goal — tragedy's *catharsis* and *nāṭya*'s *rasa*. It could be useful to compare Aristotle's definition of tragedy and its six parts with *nāṭyaśaṁgraha* and its eleven components in *Nāṭyaśāstra* (VI.10). The comparison of the Oriental expressive poetics of drama and the emotive factor in Greek tragedy is much more important than it is usually thought to be. The theory of *rasa* reveals the complexity of the artistic process which leads to the aesthetic goal of *rasa*; the interpretation of *catharsis* must take into account a variety of different things such as pleasure, learning, and the physical, cognitive and ethical aspects of the emotions. All these elements should be put into the context of the performance, as in

Nāṭyaśāstra. One should not forget the connection between structure of the dramatic text with the aesthetic goal.

Epilogues could be described as a kind of a theatrical metaphor or as a kind of a "metatheatrical" consciousness, a self-referential quality through which the play calls attention to its own function as a theatrical performance.

Further comparative research on the similarities, as well as differences between these two theatrical traditions could be very useful for our understanding of these performing arts.[28]

The above-mentioned analogies do not prove that tragedy influenced *nāṭya* and vice versa.[29]

I shall point to some important differences without elaborating upon them. It would require a thorough analysis of each mentioned item:

– There is no chorus in *nāṭya*.
– It was popular to bring *yavanikā* as a proof of Greek influence but we have no conclusive proof concerning the origin of word *yavanikā* – it may mean Ionian or Greek material. As how was it used is unclear we find it as in the words *antaryavanikā*[30] and *bahiryavanikā*[31] on *pūrvaraṅga* in the Vth *ādhyāya* of *Nāṭyaśāstra*. Something similar to *pūrvaraṅga* does not exist in Greek tragedy.

---

28 Indian authors of whom I know that wrote on the comparison between Greek and Indian theatre (G.K. Bhat, R.L. Singal and Bharat Gupt) I do not cite because I have a different approach to the subject. The book of Asha Saxena is unavailable to me. I have no information about further work of Indian authors on the subject.

29 Bansat-Boudon (1992: 11) also thinks that the hypothesis of a Greek influence is unacceptable.

30 Gönc Moačanin 2011: 123-36.

31 Gönc Moačanin, forthcoming.

- The architecture: Greek *theatron* for great audience is incomparable with a small *nāṭyamaṇḍapa* as described in the second chapter of *Nāṭyaśāstra.* Whether it ever existed remains to be proved. In my article "Nāṭyamaṇḍapa: A Real or Fictional Performing Space of the Classical Indian Theatre"[32] I have argued that most probably theatre as special edifice never existed because there was no need for it as dramas were performed in open on the occasions of *utsava*s or in the palaces. The detailed description of *nāṭya-maṇḍapa* follows the rules of Śāstric literature and in it I see a small Vāstuśāstra incorporated into *Nāṭyaśāstra*. Some of the parts of Greek theatre were *parodoi* (gateways), *orchestra* (a circular dancing place for chorus), *skene* (the stage building); there was use of mechanical devices as *ekkyklema* (a wheeled platform), *mechane* (crane), etc.
- Difference of masks: Actors wore masks and *cothurnus* (a high thick-soled boot or buskin worn by actors).
- Difference of public participation and social organization: The Greek *polis* theatre was for general public. In *nāṭya* educated public could only follow the performance.
- Different world-view:[33] *Nāṭya* belonged to the Hinduistic world-view and according to the aesthetics of *kāvya śṛṅgāra rasa* was of utmost importance and happy end was expected; the goal was emotional harmony. In Greek tragedy there is no happy ending, *catharsis* seems to imply transformation of painful and destructive emotions of pain and pity into the pleasure associated with insight (*anagnorisis*). Other important concepts of Greek tragedy are *hamartia* or tragic flaw and *hubris*, difficult term to explain but it can be said that it is concerned with the honour and shame of the individual.

---

32 Gönc Moačanin 2003: 29-37.

33 Cf. Swann 1969: 118.

Let me conclude with some of the analogies. In my view without the existence of the epics (*Mahābhārata* and *Rāmāyaṇa*) Indian classical dramatic theatre would not have assumed the shape of *nāṭya*. The question of the origin of *nāṭya* is directly connected with the complex question of the formation of the epics and it was in the epics that I see the main turning point that shows the way from ritual theatre to dramatic classical theatre. *Nāṭyaśāstra* itself says that *nāṭya* is made along with Itihāsa (I.119). That may mean that the text which was Itihāsa had been transposed into *itivṛtta* in *nāṭya* (i.e. what had been said became what happened) with a help of a very complicated dramaturgical procedure and it was done in the form of *vācikābhinaya*, with the help of other *abhinayas*, presented on the stage.[34]

Greek tragedy also found its sources in Homeric epic poems and in epic cycles with Trojan and Theban themes. As Robert Pignarre said, epic gave a ferment to drama, but that does not imply that dramatic art can be reduced to the simple mime based on the epic.[35]

Nāṭya used stories from Purāṇas and from *Bṛhatkathā* also. There was also an impact of lyric poetry and prose literature. Tragedy embraces choral song, solo lyrics, elegiac and iambic poetry. Dramatic theatre grows as a creative amalgam of existing forms and not as a totally mysterious and unparalleled new thing whose origins require to be investigated upon.[36] Besides, classical theatrical forms were the invention of gifted artists, a phenomenon that took its form at some definite place and time, embracing social, aesthetic, psychological and other factors. Greek tragedy had its Thespis, and later Aeschylus; tragedy was born in Athens in the time of Pisistratus and flourished in Pericles' Athens of the fifth century BCE. With the appearance of the actor we come to the threshold of the dramatic theatre. In Greece we know that Thespis was the first actor but for

---

34 Gönc Moačanin 1999: 247.

35 Robert Pignarre 1959: 13.

36 Gönc Moačanin 1999: 246.

nāṭya we know of no time and no place for its beginnings, and no inventor, because, as we learn from *Nāṭyaśāstra*, everything happened in the realms of gods. Though, it is worth noting that the legendary author of *Nāṭyaśāstra* was Bharata — an actor.[37] I agree with J.-P. Vernant[38] that Greek tragedy was an invention, I add that *nāṭya* was also an invention.

We may sometimes find answers to how something happened in dramatic art, but can we tell why it happened as it did? We would be aware of the fact that the plays are not museums where everything has its place and explanation. Dramas may preserve features dating from the remote past, not because these features are old and interesting, but because they were useful in some way for the creators of specific arts.[39]

At the end, I would like to say that most theories dealing with influence and/or origins of *nāṭya* rarely refer to *Nāṭyaśāstra* without which there is no real understanding of *nāṭya*. And as for the influence or influences the language barrier was not taken account of.

The difficult and unsolved problem of the influence of Greek tragedy remains open[40] and should be reopened. I hope that I have pointed to some of the aspects of both theatrical traditions which are worth of further research. It is a very complex subject and, better to understand it, a team work is needed consisting of experts in *nāṭya* and in antique theatre which should be presented historically in their different aspects. Finally, all the existing theories about the influences should be reconsidered anew in the light of present knowledge of the past theatrical traditions.

---

37 Gönc Moačanin 2003: 243.

38 Vernant 1989: 13.

39 Gönc Moačanin 1999: 247.

40 Bronkhorst 2003: 807 also thinks that the Greek influence still awaits a serious critic.

References

Bansat-Boudon, L., 1992, *Poétique du théâtre indien: Lectures du Nāṭyaśāstra*, Paris: Publications de l'École Française d'Extrême-Orient.

Bernard, P., 1978, "Communication: Campagne de fouilles 1976-1977 à Aï Khanoum (Afghanistan)", *Comptes-rendus des séances de l'Académie des Inscriptions et Belles-Lettres*, 122 année, N. 2, pp. 421-63.

Bronkhorst, J., 2003, "Sylvain Lévi et les origins du théâtre indien", *Asiatische Studien – Études Asiatiques*, **LVII**(4): 793–811.

Goblet d'Alviella, 1926 (1897), *Ce que l'Inde doit à la Grèce*, Paris: Paul Geuthner.

Gönc Moačanin, K., 1999, "Nāṭya versus the Epic Literature: Some Questions About Relationships Between Classical Indian Theatre and the Mahābhārata, Rāmāyaṇa, Harivaṁśa and Some Pūrāṇas" in *Composing a Tradition: Concepts, Techniques and Relationships, Proceedings of the First Dubrovnik International Conference on the Sanskrit Epics and Purāṇas 1997*, ed. Mary Brockington and Peter Schreiner, Zagreb Croatian Academy of Sciences and Arts, pp. 245-56.

———, 2002, *Izvedbena obilježja klasičnih kazališ nih oblika: grčka tragedija — indijska nāṭya — japanski nō* (Theatrical Practice of Classical Theatrical Forms: Greek Tragedy — Indian *nāṭya* — Japanese nō), Zagreb: Hrvatsko filološ ko druš tvo (English summary pp. 256-60).

———, 2002, "The Nāṭyaśastra as a (Distorting?) Mirror to the Epic/Purāṇic Mythic Image: The Question of Its Dating" in *Stages and Transitions: Temporal and Historical Frameworks in Epic and Purāṇic Literature, Proceedings of the Second Dubrovnik International Conference on the Sanskrit Epic and Purāṇas 1999*, ed. Mary Brockington, Zagreb: Croatian Academy of Sciences and Arts, pp. 221-38.

———, 2003, "Nāṭyamaṇḍapa: A Real or a Fictional Performing Space of the Classical Indian Theatre", *Nagoya Studies in Indian Culture and Buddhism: Saṁbhāṣa*, **23**: 29-37.

———, 2003, "The Origin(s) of Nāṭya: Nāṭya versus Ritual", *Cracow Indological Studies*, **IV-V**: 239-50.

———, 2011, "Antaryavanikā: The Musical Part of Pūrvaraṅga" in *Interrelations of Indian Literature and Arts*, ed. Lidia Sudyka, Cracow: Ksiegarnia Akademicka, pp. 123-36.

———, 2013, "Does Śāstric Literature Use Stylistic Devices?: The Example of the *Nāṭyaśāstra* in *Stylistic Devices in Indian Literature and Art*, ed. G. Boccali and E. Mucciarelli, Milano: Cisalpino, pp. 97-105.

———, (forthcomming) "Nāṭyaśāstra's Pūrvaraṅga: Ritual or a Part of Nāṭya's Performance?" (to be published in the Proceedings of the 13th WSC in Edinburgh, 2006).

Jairazbhoy, R.A., 1963, *Foreign Influence in Ancient India*, Bombay: Asia Publishing House.

Karttunen, Klaus, 1997 "India and the Hellenistic World", *Studia Orientalia*, **83**, Helsinki.

Keith, A.B., 1970 (1924), *The Sanskrit Drama in Its Origin: Development, Theory and Practice,* Oxford: Oxford University Press.

Kuiper, F.B.J., 1979, *Varuṇa and Vidūṣaka: On the Origin of the Sanskrit Drama*, Amsterdam–Oxford–New York: North-Holland Publishing Co.

Lévi, Sylvain, 1890, *Le Théâtre Indien*, Paris: Emile Bouillon, 1890.

Lindenau, M., 1913, *Beiträge zur altindischen Rasalehre, mit besonderer Berücksichtigung des Nāṭyaśāstra des Bharata Muni*, Leipzig: Druck von G. Kreysing.

———, 1914, "Spuren Griechischen Einflusses im Schauspielbuch (Nāṭyaśāstra) des Bharata Muni?" in *Festschrift Ernst Windisch*, Leipzig: Otto Harrassowitz, pp. 38-42.

The Oxford Companion to Classical Civilization, 2004, ed. Simon Hornblower and Anthony Spawforth, Oxford and New York: Oxford University Press.

The Oxford Companion to Classical Literature, 2005, 2nd edn., ed. M.C. Howatson (1st edn. 1937), Oxford: Oxford University Press.

The Oxford Dictionary of the Classical World, 2005, ed. John Roberts, Oxford : Oxford University Press.

Pignarre, R., 1959, *Histoire du Theâter*, Paris: PUF.

Swann, D.L., 1969, "Incdian and Greek Drama: Two Definitions" in *Comparative Drama*, **3**(2): 110-20.

Vernant, J.-P., 1989 (1972), "Le moment historique de la tragédie en Grèce: quelques conditions sociales et psychologiques" in *Mythe et tragédie en Grèce ancienne*, by Jean-Pierre Vernant and Pierre Vidal-Naquet I, pp. 13-17, Paris: Éditions de la Découverte.

Windisch, E., 1920, "Der griechische Einfluss im indischen Drama" in *Geschichte der Sanskrit-Philologie und Indischen Altertumskunde*, vol. 2, Berlin and Leipzig: Vereinigung wissenschaftlicher Verleger Walter de Gruyter & Co., pp. 398-405.

Winternitz, M., 1968 (1920), *Geschichte derIndischen Literatur*, vol. 3, Stuttgart: K.F. Koehler Verlag.

5

Nāṭyaśāstra and Traditional Theatres of South India

Gajanan Hegde

THE Indo-Āryan and Indo-Draviḍian form two major groups amongst Indian linguistic families. South Indian languages like Tamil, Telugu, Kannada and Malayalam belong to the second group. They have been in vogue in the states of Tamil Nadu, Andhra Pradesh, Karnataka and Kerala. We find the following dance-dramas – *yakṣagāna* in Karnataka, *melatturu bhāgavatamelā* (specially in the Mellattur village of Tamil Nadu) and *kucipuḍi bhāgavatamelā* in the village Kuchipuḍi of Andhra Pradesh. In *melatturu bhāgavatamelā* the languages used are Tamil and Telugu.

Also, there are forms of theatre where Sanskrit is prominently used. These are – *kūṭiyāṭṭam*, *naṅgiyārkūttu*, and *kṛṣṇanāṭṭam* in Kerala; where three forms – *bhāgavatamelā*, *yakṣagāna* and *kucipuḍi bhāgavatamelā* – have developed through the medium of regional languages. However, all these forms very much depend on Sanskrit sources, especially on the texts like the *Nāṭyaśāstra* of Bharata, the *Abhinayadarpaṇa* of Nandikeśvara, the *Hastalakṣaṇadīpikā* of an unknown author of Kerala and the *Bharataśāstra* of Venkatasundara with regard to stagecraft, techniques, literature and the style of composition. The *Hastalakṣaṇadīpikā* was printed in Malayalam. Now it is available in Nāgarī script. *Bharataśāstra* was compiled at Mysore and was printed in Kannada script in 1901.

Bharata has defined *pada* as a metrical composition with the fixed numbers of syllables, and pauses with defined beatings and rhythm (*NŚ* XXXII.31). This definition of *pada* by Bharatamuni is followed in the literary compositions for the south Indian dance-dramas, viz. *prasaṅga* of *yakṣagāna* and *bhāgavatamelā*. The songs sung in *kṛṣṇanāṭṭam* are called *kṛṣṇagīti*s. These *kṛṣṇagīti*s are also *pada*s as per Bharata's definition. Normally *ekatāla* with 4 4 4 4 syllables is used in these *gīti*s. The following *pada* from *kṛṣṇagīti*, sung in *kṛṣṇanāṭṭam*, can be cited as an example:

mahitavaṁśo vihitajāte
ratirahote kathama kārye
kathaya caurye malinakārye
tanaya cāsmin paramamānye

Similar is the use of *pada* in *yakṣagāna-prasaṅga* (the text for *yakṣagāna*). For example:

nīrajanayane sudhāṁśuvadane
sāmajagamane tapasvinī
manmathaśarasaṁpiṇḍito 'smi
miśraya tava vācam mama vāci

According to Bharata the dramatic performances of Draviḍadeśa (south India) abound in *nāṭya* (theatre), *nṛtya* (dances) and *vādya* (percussions) along with *kaiśikī vṛtti* marked with grace and melody.[1]

The accuracy of Bharata's judgement on the taste and aptitude of the south Indian performers is validated by several dance-dramas that have been in vogue in Draviḍian land. They are full of music, songs and *kaiśikī vṛtti*.

All of these dance-dramas begin with *pūrvaraṅga* (preliminaries), which is also called *sabhālakṣaṇa* or *sabhāvandane* in some forms of

---

[1] *tatra dākṣiṇātyas tāvad bahunṛttagītavādyāḥ kaiśikīprāyāḥ caturamadhuralalitāṅgābhinayaś ca* (*NŚ* XIII prose after kārikā 36).

south. *Sūtradhāra*s in these dance-dramas have different names. *Sūtradhāra* is called *bhāgavata* in *yakṣagāna*, whereas the nomenclature *sūtradhāra* is retained in *melatturu bhāgavatamelā*, *kucipuḍi bhāgavatamelā* and *kūṭiyāṭṭam*. If *sūtradhāra* appears with costume and make-up he is called *nāndīsūtradhāra* in *kūṭiyāṭṭam*.

In *pūrvaraṅga* as performed in these dance-dramas, we find the reflection of various items of *pūrvaraṅga* as described by Bharata, viz. *pratyāhāra*, *avataraṇa*, *āśrāvaṇā*, *vakrapāṇi*, *parighaṭṭanā*, *saṅghoṭanā*, *mārgāsārita*, etc. Beside, the following fundamental rule is also practised in all these forms, especially in *yakṣagāna* and *kucipuḍi*:

kaṇṭhen ālambhayed gītam[2]
hastena artham pradarśayet ǀ
cakṣuṣā darśayed bhāvam
hastābhyām tālaṁ ācaret ǀǀ

The performer should sustain the song in the throat, should show its meaning by hands, should express the mood through the eyes and should exhibit *tāla* through feet.

In fact, this brings out a holistic design and complete perspective giving delight to the connoisseurs.

I have observed the artists of *kuchipuḍi bhāgavatamelā* practising a mute singing of the songs; this is *ālamba*. The artists of *yakṣagāna* start the first word of the poem loudly; this is *ārambha*.

In *yakṣagāna* normally the actor starts by uttering the first word of the poem. Then exhibits the hand-gestures to visualize the meaning of the words, then he starts dancing in accordance with the beats of *tāla*s.

The artists of the above-mentioned dance-dramas rely upon *Nāṭyaśāstra*, *Abhinayadarpaṇa* and *Hastalakṣaṇadīpikā* when it comes

[2] *āsyena ālambhayed gītam* is variant reading in *Abhinayadarpaṇa* of Nandikeśvara.

to the exhibition of hand-gestures.

In *yakṣagāna* and *bhāgavatamelā*, various kinds of *dhruvā* songs are sung during the course of a performance. *Praveśikī dhruvā* is the entry song. It is called *praveśapadā* in *yakṣagāna* and *praveśadāru* in *bhāgavatamelā*. The definition of *prāveśikī dhruvā* as given in *Nāṭyadarpaṇa* of Rāmacandra and Guṇacandra is followed.

Kautuka, also called *kauta* or *kūṭa* (a form of pure dance), is practised in *yakṣagāna*, *bhāgavatamelā* and *kucipuḍi*. In fact, *kautuka* is the short form of *gaṇapatikautukam*.

Kautukam is defined in *Bharatārṇava*, *Bharataśāstra* and *Bharatakośa*. Accordingly, it is based on *rāga* and *tāla* and is accompanied with recitation of *stuti* related to some deity. According to the definition quoted by *Bharatakośa*, *kauta* has four lines in *ekatāla*.

yat kiñcita tālasaṁbaddhaṁ
devatāviṣayātmakam
vicitrapāṭhasaṁyuktam
śabdārthiar upaśobhitam
kautam tat

Bharatakośa quotes a verse:

pāṭhākṣaratātparyāt
yat syāt pādacatuṣṭaye
tat kautam iti vijñeyam . . .
. . . kūṭanāmakam

Half of the verse (poem) is composed with *pāṭhākṣras* (syllables for chanting). It is called *dastu* or *bai* in *yakṣagāna* and *sollu kuttu* in *bharatanāṭyam*. The verses for *kauta* are composed in *ekatāla* and *āditāla*.

All the four types of *abhinaya* – *āṅgika*, *vācika*, *sāttvika* and *āhārya* – are adopted in the Draviḍian dance-dramas as their own style. The seven *tālas* – *dhruva*, *maṭṭhya*, *rūpakatāla*, *jhampatāla*, *tripuṭatāla*, *aṣṭatāla* and *ekatāla* – which are mentioned in *Bharataśāstra* (compiled by Venkatasundara in Kannada script) as under:

dhruvo maṭhyo aṣṭarūpakaś ca
jhampā tripuṭam eva ca
aṣṭatālaikatālau ca
saptatālāḥ prakīrtitāḥ

These are practised in Draviḍian dance-dramas. The *pāṭhākṣara* of Sanskrit dramaturgy, which means meaningless words, which are the features of *tāla*s like *dhi dhi kiṭa,* etc. are called *sollukaṭṭu* in *bhāgavatamelā* and *kuchipudi, dastu* in *yakṣagāna,* and *vāyatārī* in *kathakali, kūṭiyāṭṭam* and *nāṅgiyārakūttu.*

Bharata has divided the ornaments into four categories namely:

1. *Āvedhya* (piercing) – the ear-rings (*karṇakuṇḍala*) and nose stud of *yakṣagāna* come under this category.
2. *Bandhanīya* (tied up) ornaments like *bhujakīrti* and *edakeṭṭu* of *yakṣagāna, toluvala* and *channauram* of *kūṭiyaṭṭam;* also of *kṛṣṇanāṭṭam* type.
3. *Prakṣepya* (worn) like *kirīṭa* in *yakṣagāna* and *kūṭiyāṭṭam.*
4. *Āropya* (put round).

In the south Indian Draviḍian dance-dramas we can see all the four types of ornaments.

One can enjoy the humorous sentiment by the portrayal of *vidūṣaka* (*hasyāgāra* or *hasigadu*) by grotesqueness of costume, make-up, abnormal dance, quaint walking and funny dialogues. Bharata defines *vidūṣaka* in the following way:

vāmano danturaḥ kubjo
dvijanmā vikṛtānanaḥ
khalatiḥpiṅgalākṣaśca
sa vijñeyo vidūṣakaḥ
— *NŚ* XXXV.57

Bharata defines *hāsya rasa,* which is enacted by *vidūṣaka:*

viparītālaṁkārair
vikṛtācārabhidhānaviṣaiś ca
vikṛtair arthaviśeṣaiḥ
hasatīti rasaḥ smṛto hāsyaḥ
— *NŚ* VI.49

This image of *vidūṣaka* is reflected in *hasyāgāra* of *yakṣagāna*, *hasigadu* of *kucipuḍi bhāgavatamelā*.

Regarding the costume of *vidūṣaka* in *kūṭiyāṭṭam*, N.P. Unni says:

> *Vidūṣaka* is dressed in a very antiquated fashion with his crimson cloth turban having its golden rim and silk embossments in the centre. He also wears rolled betel leaf in one of his ears and a bunch of red flowers in the other.[3]

In this way, the techniques of Bharata's *Nāṭyaśāstra* have been appropriated in the Dravidian dance-dramas. The conceptual framework remains intact despite regional variations.

[3] N.P. Unni, *Sanskrit Dramas of Kulaśekhara*, p. 179.

Kūṭiyāṭṭam

Kṛṣṇanāṭṭam

A character of Melatturu bhāgavatamelā yakṣagāna

Māgadha — A character of yakṣagāna

Vidūṣaka of yakṣagāna

A standing style of yakṣagāna

6

Some Significant Variants in the Rasa and Bhāva Chapters as Recorded in the Newari Manuscripts

Anvita Sharma

THE problem of understanding the textual tradition of Nāṭyaśāstra and to determine its nature has been taken up not only by modern scholarship but it was equally in the minds of a few ancient *ācārya*s also. Abhinavagupta refers to his predecessor who had the view that some of the portions of *Nāṭyaśāstra* were composed by Bharata's disciples. Likewise Abhinavagupta also refers to variants in the text of *Nāṭyaśāstra*. In post-Abhinavagupta times also, there are certain references to this problem here and there. Hence, the task of preparing the critical edition of *Nāṭyaśāstra* has occupied the attention of modern scholars. But, as the entire manuscript material available so far could not be examined together with all published standard editions of the text, this task remains unaccomplished. I have been fortunate enough to be associated with the project first sponsored by Kalidasa Akademi, Ujjain (India) and now undertaken by Indira Gandhi National Centre for the Arts (IGNCA), Eastern Regional Centre, Varanasi and could have access to the photocopies of a few unutilized Newari manuscripts of *Nāṭyaśāstra* obtained under this project from Nepali (courtesy: Darbar Library, Kathmandu). While working on the chapters on *rasa* and *bhāva* (VI and VII) of *Nāṭyaśāstra*, I have come across a number of very important variants of the text which may throw some light on the text tradition as well as its nature. The present paper attempts to discuss a few of the textual variations.

A few details of the manuscripts on the basis of which I have made my studies of the text of VIth and VIIth chapters of *Nāṭyaśāstra* are being given:

1. The manuscript No. DBI 215, 6, 5 bearing the title "Nāṭyaśāstram" contains 257 folios in a palm-leaf manuscript. It has been written in Bhujimol script and a dated one. According to its colophon it was completed on the full moon-day of Kārttika, Nepali Saṁvat 344, Thursday. Nepali Saṁvat started in CE 879. Thus, the date of this palm-leaf manuscript comes to CE 1223.
2. Second manuscript No. 305 chronologically contains 381 folios written in Bhujimol script and dated as 480 Nepali year; accordingly completed in CE 1359. It was written in Lalitpur – modern Pāṭan, a city near Kathmandu – and is clearly readable. The scribers are Ānanda and Ramananta Rāma. It was written on the occasion of *rāmārka nṛtya* performance at the instance of the ruler Yaśakīrti Rāma.
3. Chronologically third manuscript No. 308 was written in clear Newari in 767 Nepali year and completed in CE 1646 and the scribers are Vinoda and Ānanda.
4. Chronologically fourth manuscript 5, 1070 was written in Devanāgarī script and copied in 947 Nepali year from the manuscript written in 480 Nepali year at the order of General Bhimsen. Accordingly this manuscript bears the date as CE 1817.
5. Other three manuscripts were written in Newari. Out of these, two are complete with thirty-five chapters and one is incomplete and ends abruptly with XXXIInd chapter.

It is clear that the oldest manuscript was written in CE 1223 and all others belong to the corpus of the oldest available manuscript material and comparable to that which was available to Abhinavagupta. Thus, this Nepali manuscript stands to be oldest dated manuscript of *Nāṭyaśāstra* whose tradition has been preserved in Nepal.

A few important facts come up on account of the manuscripts mentioned above:

1. Nepali version of *Nāṭyaśāstra* is available to us from the first quarter of the thirteenth century to the first quarter of the nineteenth century CE. It is also important that out of the seven manuscripts mentioned above, four are dated and three mention the names of the copyists also.
2. The theory and practice aspects of *Nāṭyaśāstra* were going hand-in-hand in Nepali as is evident from a reference in one of the manuscripts that was prepared on the occasion of *rāmārka nāṭya*.
3. The Nepali version comprises of thirty-five chapters and the sequential order of the chapters has been different from those of the Bombay and Baroda editions.
4. It is remarkable that some of the important readings show some affinity between the version which was before Abhinavagupta when he was writing *Abhinavabhāratī* and the version offered by the Nepali manuscripts.

Now let me discuss some of the select variant readings of VIth and VIIth chapters of *NŚ* as they appear in Nepali version.

A large number of reading variants are available in the sixth and seventh chapters of the text, which form the core text for the masters of Indian poetics who discussed the central theory of *rasa* and *bhāva*. Because of the popularity among the scholars all over the country and because of the complexity of the issues such as *rasa* and *bhāva*, the availability of the numerous readings appears to be quite natural in a tradition of a predominantly oral transmission of the Śāstra. However, preservation of this very old version of the text may be helpful in resolving some of the most debated and complex reading variants. It is not possible to discuss all the good readings occurring in this version here. I am citing a few important variants. The first is from chapter VI, verse 6, which reads as follows:

na śakyam asya nāṭyasya
gantum antaṁ kathañcana,
kasmād bahutvāj jñānām
śilpānām cāpyanantataḥ.

1. *na śakyam asya*: N-1-7, Regnaud (Variant), Grosset, GOS, KM

   śakyam iha: Regnaud, Grosset (Variant), Kashi, MMG

   Both the readings may be correct. However, the reading accepted in Nepali version may be more plausible, for reading in this version refers to the inexhaustible nature of the discipline in hand with more intimate form of pronoun *idam* in neuter, genitive, singular.

2. *gantum antaṁ*: N-1-7, Regnaud, Grosset, KM, GOS, MMG

   gantum antaḥ: Regnaud (Variant), Grosset (Variant)

   These two different readings are also correct, the first occurring in Nepali version and accepted in the majority of editions and the other recognized by Regnaud's manuscript and Grosset's manuscript – A. The first emphasizes the impossibility of crossing over the ocean-like Śāstra and the other underscores the impenetrability of Śāstra.

3. *kathañcana*: N-1-7, Regnaud, Grosset, KM, GOS, MMG

   kadācana: Regnaud (Variant), Grosset (Variant)

   Here also both the readings are meaningful. First recognized in the Nepali version and accepted by the majority of manuscript refers to the impossibility of the crossing over ocean-like Śāstra,"by any means" (*kathañcana*) and the other "in any time". However, the majority reading is preferable.

kasmād: N-1-7, Regnaud (Variant A, B), Grosset, Kashi, KM, GOS (k), MMG

yasmad: Regnaud

The reading accepted in the Nepali version raises the question why it is not possible to cross over, whereas the reading accepted in Regnaud edition offers the reply without raising the question. Hence the Nepali reading is the correct and Regnaud reading may be rejected.

bahutvāj jñānāṁ: N-1-7, Regnaud (Variant B), Grosset, GOS, Kashi, MMG

bahutvād bhāvānāṁ: KM, Grosset (Variant), GOS (Variant),

bahutvājñānāṁ: Grosset (Variant B)

bahutvājñānāṁ: Grosset (Variant g)

Here the reading occurring in Nepali version is correct grammatically for it conforms to the *sandhi* rules and also offers the logically correct reply of the question raised, whereas other reading occurring in different editions are either grammatically noconforming to the *sandhi* rules or they do not offer the logically correct answer to the question raised by the word *kasmāt*.

cāpi antataḥ: Regnaud, GOS, Kashi, MMG

cāpi tattvataḥ: N-1-7, Regnaud (Variant B), Grosset (Variant B), GOS (Variant) KM

The first reading occurring in Regnaud, Grosset, Kashi and MMG editions is accepted by Abhinavagupta whereas the reading occurring in Nepali version offers another logical explanation for the impossibility or inaccomplishability of crossing over the ocean-like Śāstra for the arts and crafts (integral to this Śāstra), which are numerous in their essential nature.

These variations of the reading show how the text may be given by the same author with two plausible versions or it may point to the way things grow in a tradition of oral transmission. However, the reading accepted by Abhinavagupta may be preferable, for it is older.

Another example of the most important reading occurs in 15th and 16th verses of the text. The text reads:

śṛṅgārahāsyakaruṇā
vīraraudrabhayānakāḥ,
bībhatsādbhutaśāntāś ca
nava nāṭyarasāḥ-smṛtāḥ || 15 ||
ete nava rasā dṛṣṭā druhiṇena mahātmanā |

I skip over all other reading variants of the work and switch over to the second example appearing in the most important reading *nava nāṭya-rasāḥ smṛtāḥ* occurring in the 15th verse of the chapter and *nava rasāḥ* in the first half of the 16th verse.

All manuscripts of the Nepali version, the manuscript B utilized by Regnaud, B manuscript of Grasset accept the reading *nava nāṭye rasāḥ smṛtāḥ* or *nāṭya rasāḥ smṛtāḥ*, whereas remaining manuscript of the Regnaud and Grasset, Baroda, Kashi and MMG editions recognize the reading *ete hyaṣṭau rasaḥ smṛtāḥ.* This reading of the Nepali version has got immense importance, for it validates the observation of Abhinavagupta with regard to the textual tradition recognizing the nine *rasas* and the inclusion of *śānta rasa* in this scheme was available in *cirantanapustakeṣu* (the old manuscripts) before him. It is clear that the Nepali manuscripts have retained the older version.

Besides, the reading in the first half of the 16th verse clearly underscores the fact that this tradition of recognizing nine *rasas* as well as the inclusion of *śānta rasa* originates from Druhiṇa or Brahmā himself and it is not any new development. It is not an inclusion under the impact of a later tradition.

The complexity of problems faced by the scholars in establishing an authentic text of *Nāṭyaśāstra* has been candidly analysed and discussed by the veteran scholar of *Nāṭyaśāstra*, Kapila Vatsyayan in her invaluable work entitled *Bharata's Nāṭyaśāstra*.[1] She has given a vivid history of the discovery of the manuscripts of the text, its publications and its pre-text as well as co-text. She has discussed the probable nature of *NŚ* as "primary text". In this regard two sets of problems are pointed out by her. First one relates to the question of oral nature of the text and the second set of problem arises,

> when this body of creative and critical writing is transcribed and now becomes a written text.[2]

Her other remark in this connection is very much illuminating. She says:

> Manuscript reflects a transcription or a minimal reduction of an oral text or otherwise. Its many manuscripts or all transcriptions, which in the language of traditional scholarship, we call recensions.[3]

She examines further the nature of Nāṭyaśāstric text and concludes:

> The text itself, then, in its very structure, makes room for fluidity of interpretation and allows for multiple ways of understanding. — Ibid.: 38

She continues and holds the view:

> The composer of the text consciously creates a fluid text. He calls it a "Śāstra of Prayoga", i.e. theory of praxis. This seeming paradox is, in fact, a foundational principle on which his edifice is created.[4]

---

[1] Kapila Vatsyayan, *Bharata*'s *Nāṭyaśastra*, Sahitya Akademi, New Delhi, 1996.

[2] Ibid., pp. 29-30.

[3] Ibid.

[4] Ibid., p. 38.

Vatsyayan's conclusions regarding the importance of this text in the context of modern discourse on whether a text has an objective status and can it be absolute or authentic at any time are of far-reaching value. She emphatically declares:

> Its authenticity and value lie in its capacity for variants and multiple readings. Bharata appears to be conscious of the fact that there would be the probability of his text being read, interpreted and performed in a number of ways, even from diverse points of view.[5]

Thus, she not only emphasizes over the importance of the search for and the interpretations of the variant readings of such *prayogaśāstric* texts, she also opens a new dimension of understanding the Indian texts assuming a written form although initially emerging in an oral tradition. In a way. she resolves the question raised by Nilli Dolchi and Alsdorf, and so vehemently argued for the heterogeneity of Nāṭyaśāstric text by Srinivasa Ayya Srinivasan. I have examined the views of Srinivasa Ayya Srinivasan selecting a few portions of chapter VI of *Nāṭyaśāstra* analysed by him in my recently published book[6] and I have shown the weaknesses of his arguments. However, the profoundness of the perspective from which Kapila Vatsyayan approaches the textuality of *Nāṭyaśāstra* sets aside all the controversies on the question of heterogeneity of the text without directly referring to it. At the same time, this approach validates the emergence of multiple readings or the existence of implicit and explicit layers of the text. To sum up, presence of multiple reading variants of a "Prayoga Śāstra" should not lead to the conclusion that such a text is a "heterogeneous" one.

---

[5] Kapila Vatsyayan, *Bharata's Nāṭyaśastra*, Sahitya Akademi, New Delhi, 1996, pp. 38-39.

[6] *Nāṭyaśāstra meṅ Rasa aur Bhāva: Navīna Pāṇḍulipiyoṅ par Ādhārita Mūla-Pāṭhasampādana, Samīkṣā tathā Siddhānta Vivecana,* Varanasi, 2011.

It is significant that after the publication of Baroda as well as Kashi editions of *Nāṭyaśāstra*, new manuscript material has been brought into light. The discovery of new manuscripts in Newari, Bhujimol and Devanāgarī scripts from Nepal is most important, for it offers not only the oldest manuscript of *Nāṭyaśāstra* on palm leaves, but also shows the continuity of tradition in a specific region for nearly seven centuries. It is also not less insignificant a fact that some of the manuscripts have been prepared on the occasion of and for the use of performance and the performing artists. Thus, *Nāṭyaśāstra* remains as a Śāstra which was in practice all over India and Nepal, and it forms the basis of one unified tradition of Śāstra as well as performance practice.

A large number of manuscripts have been brought into light after the publication of Baroda as well as Kashi editions of *Nāṭyaśāstra*. It is worth-noticing that no new manuscript material has been utilized in the revised editions of Kāvyamālā or the reprint of Manmohan Ghosh's edition. In addition to the manuscripts used in Kāvyamālā, Baroda and Kashi editions, a fairly large number of the manuscripts have been discovered, thanks to the digitization work by IGNCA, New Delhi, at the aegis of veteran scholar of Nāṭyaśāstra and renowned art critic Kapila Vatsyayan. A systematic effort has resulted into a computerized database of manuscripts so far located in public and private libraries. An attempt is also being made to microfilm and electronically store several manuscripts of the text to facilitate further research. Vatsyayan has given an Appendix at the end of her work entitled "Bharata: The Nāṭyaśāstra"[7] based on the database of the manuscripts compiled by IGNCA consisting of details about 112 manuscripts. It would not be out of place to state that about forty manuscripts have been utilized by Ramakrishna Kavi which he claims to have obtained, but most of them are not available today for a ready reference. The

[7] Kapila Vatsyayan, *Bharata*'s *Nāṭyaśastra*, Sahitya Akademi, New Delhi, 1996.

manuscripts utilized by Regnaud, Grosset, Pandita Śivadatta and Kashi Nath Parab as well as Batukanath Sharma and Baladeva Upadhyaya may be added to this number to make the number of utilized manuscript nearly fifty or so.

It is also significant that between 1970 and 1980 a survey of the manuscripts available in Nepal was made for the Nepal German Manuscript Preservation Project in which Germany and Nepal collaborated with each other. As a result, new treasure of the manuscripts was discovered in Nepal. A number of new complete as well as incomplete manuscripts of *Nāṭyaśāstra* were discovered. As stated above, the microfilms of the first and the oldest manuscript of *Nāṭyaśāstra* was made available to Kamaleshdatta Tripathi of Banaras Hindu University by his Japanese friend and student, Hisayoshi Miyamoto. Soon after the receipt of this invaluable material, Tripathi was invited by Kalidasa Akademi, Ujjain, as Director and he undertook the project of editing the Nepali version of *Nāṭyaśāstra* and translating *Nāṭyaśāstra* afresh in 1982 for the benefit of performing artists. Kalidasa Akademi successfully obtained a few more reels of microfilm of other complete and incomplete manuscripts of *Nāṭyaśāstra* written in Bhujimol, Newari and Devanāgarī and got the photographs ready for the transcription and other related works. After years of efforts, Kalidasa Akademi was successful in obtaining the photocopies of *Abhinavabhāratī* transcribed in Devanāgarī and utilized by Ramakrishna Kavi as well as some other valuable materials scattered all over the country. Also it started the transcription of the oldest manuscript of *Nāṭyaśāstra* discovered in Nepal. Later, after the return of Tripathi to Banaras Hindu University in December 1986, the transcription and collation work of these new manuscripts could not start in Varanasi before 1990s. After his retirement from Banaras Hindu University, Tripathi was invited again by Kalidasa Akademi in 2003 but the work could not gather speed in Ujjain and when he came back to Varanasi in 2007, this project was undertaken by IGNCA, Varanasi. In the meantime, Srinivasa Rath, then Director of Kalidasa Akademi, Ujjain was kind enough to permit me for working on the VIth and VIIth chapters of *Nāṭyaśāstra* on the basis of eight Nepal Manuscripts for my Ph.D. work in the Department of Sanskrit of Banaras Hindu University. In the later years, Tripathi permitted me to be associated with his research project, which has resulted into the publication of my book in 2011.[8]

It is clear that these manuscripts represent an uninterrupted line of textual tradition of *Nāṭyaśāstra* preserved in Nepal and offer an invaluable information about not only the tradition of Druhiṇa but throw light on some important readings of *Nāṭyaśāstra* chapters VI and VII on *bhāva* and *rasa*. Hence, I feel that a deeper exploration and examination of these works in comparison with other manuscripts and the authentic editions of *Nāṭyaśāstra* would prove to be highly valuable and fruitful.

[8] *Nāṭyaśāstra meṅ Rasa aur Bhāva.*

7

Abhijñānaśākuntalam on Modern Stage

Radhavallabh Tripathi

SIR William Jones started learning Sanskrit after his arrival in Calcutta. He came to know that there were *kāvya*s (poems and plays in Sanskrit, and studied *Abhijñānaśākuntalam* (*AS*) of Kālidāsa. In 1787, he started translating *Abhijñānaśākuntalam* into English, completed the translation on 17 August 1788; and in 1789 his edition of *Abhijñānaśākuntalam* with the translation was published. This became an epoch-making event. It was the dawn of a new era,

> termed the Sacountala era by the French writer, Raymond Schwab in his *Oriental Rennaissance,* due to the unprecedented interest created by the play, bringing up a real *coup de théatre* in the history of ideas and sensibilities.[1]

Even though the translations of *Bhagavad-Gītā* and *Hitopadeśa* had just come out four years before Jones published his translation of *Abhijñānaśākuntalam*, it was really Kālidāsa's play "that truly initiated the oriental renaissance"[2] in a crucially important period of world history when the French Revolution was happening and the Romanticism was being introduced together with a new consciousness of human values. Śakuntalā appeared in this scenario to play a decisive role in the making of history. It was a miraculous

---

1 Lyne Bansat-Boudon, *The Reception of Asian Performing Arts in XVII-XXth Century Europe – The Case of France.*

2 Ibid.

discovery for Goethe, who wrote a poem on Śakuntalā. When the French scholar, Chézy sent him in *Editio Princepts of Śakuntalā* (1830) with translation and notes with the citation of Goethe's poem, Goethe, his enchantment for Śakuntalā, remaining undiminished even after forty years, thanked Chézy and wrote to him that "Śakuntalā has been a start for him that made night more pleasant than day and it had marked an epoch in his life."[3]

These renderings of *Abhijñānaśākuntalam* in eighteenth-nineteenth centuries created a new interest about Indian literary traditions in Europe.

The publication of *Abhijñānaśākuntalam* also created a worldwide interest in Indian classics and helped to usher in an era of renaissance in India also. *Abhijñānaśākuntalam* in this sense became a symbol of India's national identity.

With this, Kālidāsa was introduced on modern Indian stage. *Abhijñānaśākuntalam* was performed immediately after its first publication by Sir William Jones. The performance was presented in Calcutta theatre in 1789. The significance of this performance must be understood in the light of the fact that Calcutta theatre, ever since its inception in 1779, was producing only English plays by authors like Shakespeare till then. That it chose to perform the English translation of *Abhijñānaśākuntalam* by Sir William Jones soon after its publication shows the impact that Kālidāsa's play had created in literary circles.

Since then the play was taken up by the most eminent theatre directors in India and abroad – Radhey Shyam Kathavachak, Ebrahim Alkaji, Prathviraj Kapoor, Adya Rangacharya, Narendra Sharma, B.V. Karanth, Grotowsky, Prasanna, Subbanna, Rita Ganguli, Shyamanand Jalan and Sanakya Ebotombi are just a few to cite. This paper intends to investigate a few of its performances from the following angles:

---

[3] Lyne Bansat-Boudon, *The Reception of Asian Performing Arts in XVII-XXth Century Europe – The Case of France.*

- Kālidāsa's play as an impetus to renaissance in nineteenth century.
- Search for Indian theatre through *Abhijñānaśākuntalam*.
- Sanskrit theatre in the context of global theatre.

This also started the series of attempts at the presentation of *Abhijñānaśākuntalam* on the nineteenth-century stage in India and other countries as well. Gérard de Nerval presented an adaptation of Kālidāsa's play for the French stage around 1850.[4] In 1858, Theophile Gaurtier adopted *Abhijñānaśākuntalam* in the form of a ballet which was performed at the Opera de Paris on 14 July. Lyne Bansat-Boudon terms it "the first comeback on stage of a work that had been so far mainly praised for its poetic perfection". She also says that "the date of 14 July reinforces the hypothesis of a secret affinity between Śakuntalā and French Revolution".[5] Jules Michelet published *The Women* in 1859, in which Kālidāsa's heroine was eulogized with an advice to young ladies initiated into the joy of love to read the play.[6]

In India, some Parsi theatre companies initially attempted to put *Abhijñānaśākuntalam* on stage. The play was adapted in Urdu or Hindustani. There is a reference to a play *Śakuntalā* having been presented on stage by Haphez Mohammad in 1886. Agra Natak Mandali, established by Mirza Nazir Beg, performed *Abhijñānaśākuntalam* at Bareilley in 1899.

There are translations/renderings of *Abhijñānaśākuntalam* by veteran authors of Parsi theatre like Arama, Radhey Shayam Kathavachaka (1932) and Narayan Prasad Betab (1945).[7] Kathavachaka had scripted *Abhijñānaśākuntalam* for a Bombay film.

---

4 I am thankful to Professor Pierre Syvain Filliozat for this information.

5 Lyne Bansat-Boudon, op. cit.

6 Lyne Bansat-Boudon, op. cit.

7 Betab was supposed to be one of the greatest and most successful amongst playwrights aligned to Parsi theatre.

A great dramatist and script writer Kathavachaka, tried to bring the beauty of Kālidāsa's play in his rendering. Both Kathavachaka and Arama had scripted their adaptations in the form of dance-dramas, whereas Betab's rendering is nearer to the original and is in mixed prose and verse. All these were written for stage purpose. The script created on the basis on Kathavachaka's translation was used for a film in 1931.[8]

As Parsi theatre catered to popular taste, the attempts to put *Abhijñānaśākuntalam* were marred with vulgarity. Kunvarji Nazir was the proprietor of Vicotoria Natak Mandali, one of the pioneer theatre companies of those days. He was touring with his production of Śakuntalā between 1874 and 1876 from Calcutta to Kashi. *Kashi Patrikā,* a periodical, published the reviews of the performance on 10 June 1875, commenting that the performance did not rise up to the expectations.[9]

Bharatendu, the most outstanding poet, author and dramatist of that period in north India, and an actor and theatre director as well, who created an era (Bharatendu-yuga) by his writings and journalism in the history of Hindi literature, was in the audience. The performance was quite unpalatable for him and when the actor performing Duṣyanta started dancing with twists and turns of his waist, singing a cheap song, Bharatendu was furious and got up with his colleagues – Dr Thiebo and Babu Pramath Dash – and walked away saying, "now this is completely unbearable! They are butchering Kālidāsa!"[10]

This led to a series of good translations of Kālidāsa exploring the possibilities of their performance. Raja Lakshman Singh, one of the laureates of nineteenth-century Hindi literature, published his

---

8 *Bhāratīya Raṅgamañca kā Vivecanātmaka Itihāsa* [Agyat], p. 254.

9 *Kashi Patrika*, 30 June 1875, Q in Agyat, *Bhāratīya Raṅgamañca kā Vivecanatmaka Itihāsa*, p. 254.

10 *Bhāratendu Granthāvalī*, p. 753.

translation. Vrindavanlal Verma, a well-known Hindi novelist, remembers to have seen the performance of this translation around 1905 at Jhansi.

But neither Bharatendu's endeavours nor the performances of some of these literary translations by celebrated authors could stop the journey of Kālidāsa's masterpiece on Parsi theatre through popular renderings. One of the performances was even given before the Prince of Wales at Madras by Dadi Patel, under the banner of Original Victoria Company around 1875.

The search for Indian identity through *Abhijñānaśākuntalam* via Parsi theatre did not come to an end. The milieu still believed that a happy marriage of *Abhijñānaśākuntalam* and Parsi theatre was possible. In 1920, Maharaja Bhavani Singh of Jhālāwāḍ, a state in Rajasthan, started a very ambitious project of building a theatre in the backward city of Jhālāwāḍ. The opening of the theatre was marked by the performance of *Abhijñānaśākuntalam* itself on 16 July 1921. Female roles were played by male actors. Nanhe Khan was playing the role of Śakuntalā, Chote Khan of Kaṇva and Mirza Nazir Beg "Nazir" performed Duṣyanta. Kings from neighbouring states were invited to witness the grand opening. An inscription on marble was unveiled with a note on the performance of *Abhijñānaśākuntalam*.

Prithviraj Kapoor, a towering figure in theatre and cinema, presented his version of *Abhijñānaśākuntalam*, under the banner of Prithvi Theatres, one of the most dynamic repertoires of twentieth century. In fact, Kālidāsa's play was the debut performance by Prithvi Theatre on 9 March 1945 in the Opera House of Mumbai. The script of the play was given by Pundit Natayan Prasad "Betab". "Betab" was adamant and uncompromising on the style of Parsi theatre for the adoption.

Ujra Mumtaj, one of the most celebrated heroines of Bombay film industry performed Śakuntalā's role, Prithviraj himself appeared as Duṣyanta and his son, Shashi Kapoor, who was to be a popular hero in the coming years, played Bharata.

Through this performance, Prithviraj Kapoor wanted to align his theatre with Indian ethos and value system. A realistic touch was given to the presentation by creating scenes of royal court through wooden columns and painted walls and royal seat, and in the scene of hermitage, trees shown through cut outs of plywood. The play was presented in the style of Parsi theatre with certain improvizations and innovative designs. By using different spotlights, Kaṇva was shown witnessing the love scene between Duṣyanta and Śakuntalā. This was the first attempt to unearth a sub-text of a Sanskrit drama on modern stage. Balwant Gargi, a theatre critic, remarks that the spirit of Kālidāsa was absent from the performance.

Nine shows were consecutively given at the Prithvi Theatre itself and all in all there were about 250 repeated shows all across the country, which was rather discouraging, considering that many of the popular plays by Prithviraj Kapoor were performed more than 2,000 times each.

A production of Kālidāsa's *magnum opus* by as eminent a theatre person as Grotowski in 1960 was equally a failure, as it was "ironically aiming at showing to West the stereotyped image of Eastern theatre that it generally builds".[11]

Meanwhile there were attempts to establish the glory of theatre and as a parallel force to Bombay cinema. In 1939 Moonlight theatre was established in Calcutta by Govardhan Mehrotra. The performance of *Abhijñānaśākuntalam* under its banner was directed by Prem Shankar Narsi, one of the great actors and directors in Parsi theatre.[12]

---

[11] See Lyne Bansat-Boudon's article in this volume.

[12] See copy of the photograph on p. 125 presenting Prem Shankar Narsi (Master Fida Hussain) as Duṣyanta in this performance.

Hindustani Theatre was established by Begum Kudasia Zaidi, and after the production of the *Mṛcchakaṭikam* under its banner, Narendra Sharma (1924-), one of the leading choreographers trained in Udaishankar's Almora centre and a well-known Hindi poet, directed *Abhijñānaśākuntalam* for it. It was one of the most remarkable performances – an attempt to bring out the poetry and spirit of the play. Curtain was dropped only once – after the fourth act. In the scene of Duṣyanta's hunting in the forest, groups of trees and wild animals – deers were shown moving along. This was the technique which Bharata in his *Nāṭyaśāstra* called *sañjīva* – representing living animals on the stage. The actors created the moving forest and whole ecology.

The *Sunday Times* of 17 July 1961 carried a detailed report on this performance. The report said:

> The production had many graces. It had movement that flowed across the stage. Groups formed and broke and fell back into compositions that were marked by some inevitability. Choreography by Narendra Sharma was of good timing and finish. Décor by M.S. Sathyu was adept, stage sets well devised, lighting controlled intelligently and with sensitiveness. The sheer mechanics of the play left little to be desired.

The critic was also of all praise for the actress Archana Mohan who performed as Śakuntalā.

> She was persuasive of charm, and grace and a poetry of loving. Her movements were well modulated.

Still, the story of this performance is a mixture of success and failure. The performance was designed as dance-drama, but the script given by Niaz Haider was loaded with dialogues emphasizing situations. So that the naturalistic design was in discord with the poetic.

During 1950s and 1960s, notable amongst the performances of Kālidāsa's *magnum opus* were by Baba Dike under the banner of his Natya Bharati in 1962. Rahul Barpute, who was to become a leading journalist played Duṣyanta and Suman Dharmadhikari a well-known actress of the group performed Śakuntalā. Baba Dike adopted the translation by Viraj, which was very unsuitable for theatre performance. The audience, the director of the play and the actors all were unsatisfied with the script.[13]

Abhijñānaśākuntalam was staged by the Volos theatre group from Athens in Greek language and Greek style on 12 November 1986 on the occasion of Kālidāsa festival at Ujjain. Śakuntalā was presented by three different female artists with a view to visualize the transformation in her character. Chorus was presented in the Greek style.

Hindi translation of *Abhijñānaśākuntalam* by Mohan Rakesh was taken up by eminent theatre directors like Ibrahim Alkaji, Prasanna, Rita Ganguli, Shyamanand Jalan and Sanakya Ebotombi between 1974 to 1987.[14]

When Ibrahim Alkaji joined the National School of Drama at Delhi in 1962, he had already undergone through an important phase of his career as a theatre director at Mumbai, the performance of Dharmavir Bharati's *Andha Yuga* directed by him for Satyadev Dube's Terrace Theatre having heralded a new era in Hindi stage. Hindi translation of *Abhijñānaśākuntalam* by Mohan Rakesh was one of the earliest productions (1963-64) under his direction at the National School of Drama.

Another noteworthy performance of the *Abhijñānaśākuntalam* was under the banner of Kalidasa Academy of Allahabad around 1960. Shrikrishna Das, a veteran theatre activist organized the event. Surya Avasthi of Prayag Vidyapeeth is reported to have performed the role of Śakuntalā.[15] Tapas Sen, who acquired legendary fame

---

13 *Bhāratīya Raṅgamañca kā Vivecanātmaka Itihāsa* [Agyat], p. 298.

14 Pratibha Agrawal, ed., *Bhāratīya Raṅgakośa*, p. 187.

15 *Kālidāsīya nāṭya aur mere Raṅgānubhava* (Hindi). Kamleshdatta Tripahi *Punarnavā*, Souvenir of Akhil Bharatiya Kalidasa Samaroha, Ujjain, 2006, pp. 49-50.

for his light effects on theatre and in Bombay movies, was called from Calcutta to create light effects.

During and after the seventh decade of the twentieth century, there were attempts to establish a dialogue between theatre persons and Sanskrit scholars with a view to search the identity of Indian theatre through *Nāṭyaśāstra*.

One of the most remarkable performances of *Abhijñānaśākuntalam* was directed by Adya Rangacharya (R.V. Jagirdar), an eminent Kannada playwright and himself a scholar of Sanskrit drama and *Nāṭyaśāstra*. This performance was prepared for Kalidasa Festival at Ujjain in 1976. It was an attempt to give a faithful representation of the original play in Sanskrit with emphasis on *vācika* and correct recitation. Adya Rangacharya had edited *Abhijñānaśākuntalam* to prepare his stage version and and this script did justice to the original play. An attempt was made to render Kālidāsa's poetic beauty and aesthetic universe on stage. The play moved in slow rhythm. Karanth had given some brilliant touches saving the performance from becoming too conventional or too realistic. It was also fascinating to listen to him with his musical notes in the background. But on the whole, the performance lacked in perception and insight.

Abhijñānaśākuntalam as per the precepts of Bharata's *Nāṭyaśāstra* was made by Puru Dadhich – himself a scholar of Bharata's *Nāṭyaśāstra* and a dancer and choreographer. He presented the play at Lucknow on 31 March 1980. The play was sponsored by Hindustani Sangita Mahavidyalaya and Akhil Bharatiya Sanskrit Parishad, Lucknow.

In 1980s the play was taken up by a number of amateur repertoires. Kalaksetra of Madras gave its performance with all the perfection of Rukmini Arundel's masterpiece choreography at the Kalidasa Samaroha (festival) at Ujjain in 1985. Another theatre group devoted to Sanskrit theatre, the Goa Hindu Association performed *Abhijñānaśākuntalam* during this year on the same platform.

The emphasis shifted to the creaton of a physical stage as per the prescriptions of *Nāṭyaśāstra* when Vijya Mehta presented the Marathi translation of *Abhijñānaśākuntalam* under the banner of the Goa Hindu Association, Mumbai, in 1985. Moments of rupture came during the course of performance, but were lost in the paraphernalia. There was perfection in technique, in combinations of movements. The following stage designs from *Nāṭyaśāstra* were adopted by Vijaya Mehta: (i) *mattavāraṇī*, (ii) *kutapa* and *vedī* for seating the musicians, (iii) division between *raṅgapīṭha* and *raṅgaśīrṣaḥ*, and to a certain extent, (iv) *kakṣyāvibhāga* or imaginary zonal divisions.

In the same year (1985), Shri Simhajit Sinha, a well-known exponent of Manipuri dance presented his rendering of *Abhijñānaśākuntalam*. The performance was enlivened with rare grace and beauty. Through this performance the dance-*guru* was able to extend the frontiers of Manipuri dance form, and replenish the form with freshness of Kālidāsa's imagery.

In the Kalidasa Samaroha of 1989, Shantinath Ghosh brought his repertoire from Kolkata to present the *Abhijñānaśākuntalam*, and in 1994, S. Janaki presented *Abhijñānaśākuntalam* on the banner of Saṁskrita Raṅga, founded by her *guru* V. Raghavan.

However all these performances failed to rediscover the soul of Sanskrit theatre and to achieve a major breakthrough in the process of building up a national theatre.

Ujjain became a hub of Saṅskrit theatre, and the *Abhijñānaśākuntalam* providing invitation to emerging theatre directors for experimentations. Two young and talented artists presented *Abhijñānaśākuntalam* in original Sanskrit – Dhirendrakumar in 1992 and Rajendra Avasthi in 2004. Sanskrit theatre was resuscitated with inculcation of motifs from regional forms. Dhirendrakumar could create the new theatric universe through his *Abhijñānaśākuntalam* because he had Ustad Omprakash Chaurasia as a singer with beautiful rendering of Kālidāsa's original verses through traditional Mālwī music. Dhirendrakumar used Mālwī instead of Prākṛt in the dialogues of female and characters of lower type. He made profuse use of chorus, *raṅgapaṭṭī* and combination of forms like Paṇḍavanī, Mañca and Chāu. Shrinivas Rath had edited the Sanskrit script of *Abhijñānaśākuntalam* for Avasthi's production. Costumes from Malwa, tunes of Mālwī folk music and through imaginative use of choreography bordering on classical and embracing the regional dance forms added to the charm of this production. In 1997, Chetan Pandit, a young theatre director, presented *Abhijñānaśākuntalam* in Ujjain.[16] Yogesh Tripathi, one of the emerging theatre directors from the Baghelkhaṇḍ region of Madhya Pradesh, produced the Bagheli version of *Abhijñānaśākuntalam* under the banner of Kṣitija on 3 November 2009 for the Kalidasa Festival of Ujjain.[17]

However, with the arrival of Kavalam Narayana Panikkar's version of Kālidāsa's *magmum opus*, the whole scenario became vibrant. The debut performance was given on the stage of Kalidasa Samaroha at Ujjain on 13 November 1986. Subsequently, Panikkar himself replaced the robust and forceful voices of protest and challenge by the people or *prajā*, a mark of his first presentation, by more mellow and subtle readings of the sub-text as understood by him. The play was transformed with different designs when the audiences beheld it almost after a gap of twenty five years in 2010 at the Bharata Bhavan, Bhopal. Panikkar gave brilliant touches by a very imaginative use of *raṅgapaṭṭī*s and forms of traditional theatres of Kerala in some of the scenes. Panikkar had already made a long journey of his experimentations with Sanskrit drama and theatre. In 1978, his production of *Madhyamavyāyoga* formed a moment of

---

16 These facts are based on the article of Shailendra Kumar Sharma in the Souvenir of Akhil Bharatiya Kalidasa Samaroha, Ujjain, 2006, pp. 51-58.

17 These facts are taken from the Souvenir of Kalidasa Festival, 2009 published by Kalidasa Saskriti Akademi, Ujjain.

history in this journey, after which he presented *Karṇabhāram* and *Ūrubhaṅgaṁ*. His experiments of presenting the relationships between the individual and groups on stage found a fine expression in his production of *Abhijñānaśākuntalam*. Panikkar interpreted the whole text as an exposition of relations between the king and his subjects. The group of helpers in the hunting (*mṛgayā*) of Duṣyanta turn out to become the representatives of the people when the hunting for animals assumes the proportions of the hunting for human beings.

Pannikar's *Abhijñānaśākuntalam* has become a memorable experience because of his very imaginative use of *raṅgapaṭṭī*s (movable curtains). He could exhibit these movable curtains in as symbols of the trauma, inner conflicts and the psychic experiences of the characters of *Abhijñāśākuntalam* bringing out the inner core of the play.

Meanwhile, Sanakya Ebotombi presented a delicate and delightful version of *Abhijñānaśākuntalam* in Manipuri style.

Even a cursory view of the performances of *Abhijñānaśākuntalam* beginning from 1789 to 2012 confirms the fact that the masterpiece of Kālidāsa has never been just a drama and the performances were not given only for entertainment. Why should a *mahārājā* in a remote state in Rajasthan invite a troupe to perform *Abhijñānaśākuntalam* for the premiere show of the newly-built theatre house? Why Prithviraj Kapoor after the series of hilarious performances of his dramas like "Deewar" or "Pathan" – which were enormous hits at the "box office" and created records in the number of enraptured audiences – should turn to Kālidāsa's play and insist that the translation should be nearest to the spirit of the classic and evince Indian values?

Rashtriya Sanskrit Sansthan in its annual festival of Sanskrit Drama where ten troupes every year from its campuses participate, made a different kind of experiment with *Abhijñānaśākuntalam* in 2011. All the seven acts were performed successively by seven different troupes.

Abhijñānaśākuntalam, in fact, helped in the search of national identity as well as the theatrical identity of India. The failures in its performances are also symbolic to our search for our own identity.

To whom should we ascribe the responsibility of the failures in performing *Abhijñānaśākuntalam?* To Kālidāsa, who soars high in the sky of imagination and delights us by his poetry but creates problems for putting the drama up on the stage; or to the directors who made attempts to present his play through their own fancies and failed to grasp the inner core of the original playwright; or to the performers who were inept in creating the subtle imagery, the complicated moods of the characters and the world of emotions, or to the audiences who were not properly trained to rise from their own level to be able to travel to the pinnacles to which the play journeys? It is true that *Abhijñānaśākuntalam* has always been a challenge, and will remain a challenge.

Acknowledgement

I am extremely grateful to Natranga Pratishthan, New Delhi, and its Secretary, Rashmi Bajpeyi, for providing some photographs and copy of the news reporting of *Abhijñānaśākuntalam* staged under the banner of Hindustani Theatre, to Kalidasa Akademi, Ujjain, and P.N. Shastri for giving photographs of the performance by Volos theatre from Greece.

References

Agrawal, Pratibha (ed.), 2005, *Bhāratīya Raṅgakośa*, pt. I, New Delhi: National School of Drama.

——— (ed.), 2006, *Bhāratīya Raṅgakośa*, pt. II, New Delhi: National School of Drama.

Punarnavā, Souvenir of Akhil Bharatiya Kalidasa Samaroha, Ujjain, 2006.

Smārikā, Souvenir of Akhil Bharatiya Kalidasa Samaroha, Ujjain, 1986.

Śakuntalā in Holland

Śakuntalā in Polland

Group – Maharshtra–Mumbai–Brahman Sabha; play performed in National Drama Festival, 1954

Abhijñānaśākuntalm presented by students or Sringeri Campus of Rashtriya Sanskrit Sansthan in 2011.

A Scene from *Abhijñānaśākuntalm* as directed by Narendra Sharma

Shakuntala And Theatre Studies In New York

HS 15/11/59 By JOHN T. REID

IN the considerable urge of general interest for things Indian which is noticeable in the United States today, "Shakuntala", the classical drama of Kalidasa, has not been overlooked. Some weeks ago a translated version was presented in New York with a fair approximation, I am told, to the stylized beauty and colour of the original. It has generated a rather unusual amount of critical comment, all appreciative of the play, some querulous about the presentation.

"Shakuntala" also appears as one of the great books read by Columbia University undergraduates when they are enrolled in the course called "Oriental Humanities". The methods, pleasures and difficulties attendent on teaching such a course were the subject of a symposium-conference held at the University not too long ago, and the proceedings, an attractive volume entitled "Approaches To The Oriental Classics", has just reached my hands.

Among other fascinating chapters, I find in it a fresh and original essay on "Shakuntala" written by John D. Mitchell, pointing to the dramatic artistry of the play and giving a psycho-analytical interpretation of its theme. The latter, I might add, strikes me as a forced, although interesting piece of legerdemain.

Mitchell, a former professor of theatre arts at several American universities, was the U. S. delegate to the first World Conference on the Theatre, held in Bombay in 1957, under the sponsorship of UNESCO. He and his wife who was one of the founders of the American Shakespeare Festival Theatre at Stratford, Connecticut, have a wide acquaintance with the international theatre, and their interest has led them to visit scores of theatre centres all over the world.

He recently said, "After talking theatre with people in fifty countries my wife and I have found that there is a great deal Americans can learn from the foreign stage. And theatre people in other countries want to find out more about contemporary American drama".

Suiting action to words, Dr. and Mrs. Mitchell have founded, along with other prominent figures in the American drama world, the Institute for Advanced Studies in the Theatre Arts. This non-profit, privately-endowed and highly-specialized school will, when it starts operations this year, be open to high-level American professionals and students. Foreign experts from Europe and Asia will participate as teachers and staging as practised by the Comedie Francaise or the Japanese Kabuki Theatre, for example, will become accessible to serious students of the drama in New York.

All of this is exciting to those of us who are concerned with international cultural exchange, for the theatre is one of the most vivid ways in which we can learn something of the culture and ways of life of our world neighbours.

In view of Dr. Mitchell's particular interest in "Shakuntala", I will not be surprised if that fine play and other masterpieces of Indian drama eventually find their way into the curriculum offered by the Institute for Advanced Studies in the Theatre Arts.

Media reports of the performance of *Abhijñānaśākuntalm* given by Tagore Society at New York, Hindustani Samachar, 15 November 1959

Abhijñānaśākuntalam of Prithvi Theatre: Shashi Kapoor as Bharata (L) with Prithviraj Kapoor as Duṣyanta (9 March 1945)

Presentation of *Abhijñānaśākuntalam* by Volos Theatre from Greece, New York, in 1971. More pictures on pp. 117-124.

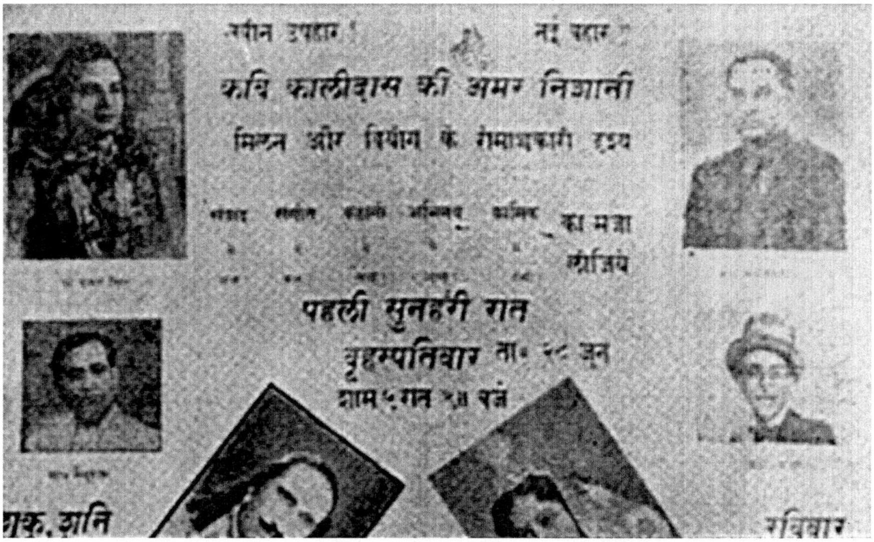

Poster showing Prem Shankar Narsi (Master Fida Hussain) in performance as Duṣyanta in *Abhijñānaśākuntalam*.

Scene from *Abhijñānaśākuntalam* as presented by Kavalam Narayan Panikkar (also on pp. 126-127)

8

Syntax of Dance Movements

Sonal Nimbkar and *Navjyoti Singh*

IN this paper we will discuss *nṛtta, nṛtya* and *nāṭya* through the movements of *manas*. Dance movement is not just an external body movement but internal as well. It is both physical and mental. Both these phenomena are different in nature. Mental phenomena, like thoughts, are sequential in nature, and they occur in time. Physical phenomena comprise movement in time and space. The externalization of thoughts requires body which utilizes space.

How does the thought that is in mind finds expression in space using body? The link between mind and body is *manas*. *Manas* connects mental and physical phenomena. It helps us to understand the internal body which plays a major role in dance. It is through body that a dancer dances. *Manas* resides and moves in the internal body. Hence tracing the movement of *manas* is essential for the construction of accurate grammar of dance. It resolves the mind–body problem.

We take a model of human as per Vaiśeṣika theory to interpret dance movement. According to this theory, human being is made up of three basic elements: *ātman* (self), *manas* (mind) and *śarīra* (body). *Ātman* with the help of *manas* makes an effort (*ceṣṭā*) on the joints of body to create dance. *Manas* is the link between *ātman* and *śarīra*. When we do a movement, *manas* goes to millions of places in the body, so if we take the gross movements of *manas* moving in the body we can know that movement. Thus understanding the movement of *manas* will help us to understand the grammar of movement. Further we will apply this understanding of *manas* in *nṛtta, nṛtya* and *nāṭya*, which will help us to understand the subtle differences in each of them accurately.

We are suggesting a four-tier model for the motion of *manas*. (A) Model of body; (B) model of motion of *manas*; (C) model of summary of the motion of *manas* (internal body sensation of affordance); and (D) model of *bhāva*s. We are making syntax of movement which integrates physical as well as mental aspect of movement.

Introduction

Dance, as the name suggests, can be understood as complex movements set to music. Every culture, every civilization has witnessed dance of one form or the other at any given point of time in history. With culture, dance has also taken different forms and evolved with time. Every region has different dance forms, which are influenced by its geography, culture, language, music, etc. When we say different dances, we are mentioning the way it is performed. That is, the movement orientation is different. Bharatanāṭyam is different from Ballet, which is different from Noh, which in turn is different from Bhāṅgṛā. These dances are different from each other not only because geographically they are located at different places or music, costume, etc. are different, but most importantly because movement orientations of each dance form is distinct from each other. For example, jumps in Bhāṅgṛā are different from *utplavan*s in Bharatanāṭyam and *sauté* in Ballet.

It is this difference that forms an important element in the syntax of dance movement. How and why is each movement different from other? How is dance movement different from non-dance movement? Can a grammar be constructed understanding movement? Can there be a universal grammar that can be applied to all the dance forms. It is this concern that this paper will address to.

Analysing Movement

Movement is an intrinsic part of any human being. It is with the movement that a toddler tries to make sense of the world around him. He twists, he turns, he hops, he runs, he talks, he walks, he slides, he bends, he sleeps, and he eats. It is with this body that he does all the movement and makes sense of himself and his surroundings. He is not only learning with his mind, he is learning with his body too. Through these movements he relates to the world within and without. As Maxine Sheets Johnstone in her book *Primacy of Movement* says: In discovering ourselves in movement and in turn expanding our kinetic reportoire of " I cans", we embark on a lifelong journey of sense-making. Thus a closer inquiry at movement will help to understand the movement and dance. This can be done in two ways: (i) pause (*sthiti*) and motion (*gati*), and (ii) postures (*sthāna*).

PAUSE AND MOTION

Each movement is a combination of pause (*sthiti*) and motion (*gati*). The pause may be for a fraction of a second but it exists. If there was no pause in a movement, it would be difficult to distinguish one movement from the another; all the movements would just coalesce. This pause can also be looked at as posture, though every pause is not a posture. For example, a walk, before one starts to walk there is a pause, the body weight is equally distributed on both the legs. To start a movement with right leg, it has to be free and light. So for this body shifts the weight that it is holding on both the legs to one leg, i.e. left. Once this movement is done, next move is to lift the leg. These two moves are distinguished with a pause. After the right leg is lifted there is a pause again and the right leg comes down on the heel and is placed on the ground. Again a pause, the right feet is flat on the floor and the left feet rolls up simultaneously. There is a pause again and the left foot is lifted up for another step and this goes on. And thus the movement continues with various combinations of pause and motion. This movement of a walk described is constructed with five pauses and five motions. Such observation of pause and motion as a phenomenological lived body experience in a movement will give a better understanding of the movement.

POSTURES

Posture is the internal sense of the body. This internal sense is the ability to recognize the position in which a limb or body is passively placed without explicitly having seen how that position is assumed by one's own body. This internal sense determines the way one moves and conducts one selves in the society and thus posture is also looked at as stance. We take deliberate stances while conducting ourselves in the society or with an individual, for example, "I will not talk to him" or "a secular stance taken by our government". There are many factors that contribute to the posture an individual has; our culture, geography, religion, thoughts, etc. to name a few. Posture is a rest or stasis in motion.

EVERY POSTURE IS STATIC AND DYNAMIC

Static posture is synchronic in nature; all the meaning the static posture conveys is available at once in moment. *Hasta-mudrās* in Indian classical dance are the classic example of this static posture. *Mudrā* is that seal which reveals the concealed meaning of a storyline. The meaning of a *hasta-mudrā* is available at once in time. It is with the help of *mudrā*s, a story is unfolded. It is the stasis of body.

Bhāva is the stasis of mind. *Bhāva* is eventual unfoldment in time; it is temporal and sequential in nature. Every posture is a reflection of *bhāva*. These postures help a *rasika* to understand *bhāva* of the character. Every (significant) posture indicates the emotion or *bhāva*, of the character portrayed by an actor (*naṭa*). In a posture *bhāva* is seen. A good posture is that which exhibits *bhāva*, emotion or a thought of the individual. For example, the walk of Bṛhannalā, a character from epic *Mahābhārata*.

Mudrā is a posture of body; *bhāva* is a posture of mind. Hence understanding of postures will help us to understand the movement structures.

This scrutiny of movement with the help of pause and motion along with postures will assist to construct the smallest unit of movement, which is the combination of pauses and motions. This smallest unit of movement will be a movement unit which is whole, one and makes sense. These are the smallest possible atomic units of movement, which cannot be bifurcated further. These atomic movements can also be understood as *karaṇa*s, which will form the basis upon which grammar will be constructed.

According to Bharata, the combination of the movements done with hand and feet is known as *karaṇa* (*hastapādasamāyogo nṛtasya karaṇaṁ bhavet*).[1]

This seems to be a very general definition. From this, it can be inferred that any dance movement is a *karaṇa*. *Adavu*, forming the basic dance steps of the Bharatanāṭyam, is also a *karaṇa* then.

Abhinavagupta further explains it by saying that combination of motion (*gati*) and pause (*sthiti*) is *karaṇa: tena gatisthitisammilitam karaṇaṁ iti ānantyaṁ.*[2]

He further says that motion is practised through *cārī*s (gait) and pause through *sthānaka*s (stances). So the next question that arises is how many pauses and motions make one *karaṇa*? Thus understanding of pause and motion along with the postures will facilitate to understand and construct *karaṇa*s. But before focusing on *karaṇa*s it is necessary to differentiate between dance and non-dance movements. Can any kind of movement become a dance movement and how?

---

1 *Nāṭyaśāstra* IV.30, p. 34, ed. and tr. Manmohan Ghosh, Varanasi: Chowkhamba Sanskrit Series, 2003.

2 Chapter IV.60, p. 291, *Bharatamuni's Nāṭyaśāstra with Commentary by Abhinavagupta*, ed. and tr. Parasnath Dwivedi, Varanasi: Sampurnananda Sanskrit Vishwavidyalaya, 1992.

Differentiating dance and non-dance movement there are two parameters that differentiate dance from non-dance movement.

1. Sauṣṭhava

Movement covers a varied range, from a walk of a toddler to highly technical and complex movement in dance. It starts with a naïve innocence and reaches its optimum fulfilment in the form of movements that shows grace, finesse and sophistication. How does this naïve innocence mature with finesse? How does this transition take place? How to understand that element which holds the key to this transformation? Each dance form may have different *sauṣṭhava* but *sauṣṭhava* is there; whereas one can carry their regular daily routine without being in *sauṣṭhava*. Etymologically *sauṣṭhava* comes from *suṣṭhu*, which means "proper" or "appropriate". It is only after one is in *sauṣṭhava* that one can begin dancing. If a dancer is not in *sauṣṭhava,* then she is not able to generate energy properly which is needed for proper execution of dance movements. Because as a dancer she has the responsibility to:

- Change the rhythm as per *tāla.*
- Execute finesse in movement.
- Communicate with the audience.

If a dancer is not in *sauṣṭhava,* then she cannot change the rhythm as quickly as the music or story demands. She has to be vigilant to the given music. Dancer also has to see that her movements are graceful. And she has to communicate with the audience. This is possible only if the first two criteria are met. *Sauṣṭhava* is the way of holding body. Even the actor or a soldier or a sportsperson is in *sauṣṭhava*. Their body is in their control. It is that state of mind from where you can execute a given task like playing a certain character or running 100 m or playing football with ease. It is that fluid state of mind from where you can take up anything upon you. You can take any character on you. That neutral state or fluid state from where you can take up any character upon you is known as *sauṣṭhava*. It makes the body light, so that there is ease and finesse in execution.

Sauṣṭhava is not just a physical condition with the body in *samapāda*, back straight, head in *sama*, hands on the waist and tummy tucked in. The *gurus* instruct their students to drill this position, so that eventually this outer physical position will gradually change the internal position. As the mind influences the body, body also influences the mind. As soon as the back straightens, state of mind changes. When feet are apart, mental state is different, they are much more relaxed but when it is in *samapāda* a dancer's body is alert. All these positions of head, feet, hand, tummy and back together kept in a certain position, dancer is in a state of awareness. It is like keeping body in neutral gear/mode, from where a dancer can move her body with ease. She has to be in that state of neutrality, fluidity. When a body is in *sauṣṭhava*, energy is better channellized. When a dancer is in *sauṣṭhava* her mind is alert, when it is not, her body is slouch, mind becomes dull. *Sauṣṭhava* helps to remain alert and stay focused.

Bharatamuni gives the following definition of *sauṣṭhava*:

> When the body is still, neither bent nor unbent, it remains at ease, with waist, ears, elbow and head in straight and even position (*samaṁ*) and breast is raised high – this position is known as *sauṣṭhava*.[3]

He advocates *sauṣṭhava* because he feels that there is no beauty (*śobhā*)[4] in a movement of dance or drama without *sauṣṭhava*.

Ashokamalla agrees with Bharata in his treatment of *sauṣṭhava* in his *Nṛtyādhyāya*.[5] Parśvanātha in his *Saṅgītasamayasāra* says that

---

[3] *NŚ* XI.90-91, p. 162, ed. and tr. Manmohan Ghosh, Varanasi: Chowkhamba Sanskrit Series, 2003.

[4] *NŚ* XI.89, ed. and tr. Manmohan Ghosh, Varanasi: Chowkhamba Sanskrit Series, 2003.

[5] *Nṛtyādhyāya* 885, p. 244, tr. Vachaspati Gairola, Delhi: Chowkhamba Sanskrit Pratishthan, 1985.

body which does not bend right, left, forward or backward is known as *sauṣṭhava*. A body does not have grace and elegance (*śobhā*) in *nāṭya* and *nṛtta* if it is without *sauṣṭhava*. *Nāṭya* and *nṛṭya* are rooted in *sauṣṭhava*:

> *gatram yadi sthitam samyak*
> *sauṣṭhavam tad udāhṛtam* ।
> *nahi sauṣṭhavahīnāṅgam*
> *śobhate nāṭyanttayoḥ*
> *nāṭyam nṛttam ca sarvam hi*
> *sauṣṭhave sampratiṣṭhitam* ।।[6]

2. The Present Body

The second condition is that the whole body of a dancer is "present" in the moment. A dancer's body is never "absent" to her. It is through this body that she responds to the rhythm, to the vocals and to the space. Each and every part of the body resonates to the given space and music. She is completely aware as to how is she lifting her leg, on what count will she lift the leg and at what distance will she again keep it on the ground. Her hands reach out to the other dancer's body or expression with compete finesse and discipline. It is through her body that she creates the architecture of movements. This is not the case for non-dance movement. An individual carries different chores throughout the day. It is with the same given body she eats, writes, reads a book and climbs the stairs. But while doing so she may not always be conscious about her body. For example, when she is eating only her mouth and her hands may be present to her, rest of the body is absent. Rest of the body recedes, disappears to her. As Drew Leder puts it:

> An absence is the being-away from itself. The lived body, as ecstatic in nature, is that which is away from itself. Yet this absence is not equivalent to simple void, a mere lack of being.

---

6 *Saṅgītasamayasāra* VII.199, ed. and tr. Acharya Brihaspati, Delhi: Bhartiya Jnanapitha, 2006.

This body remains unavailable, in the sense we are not thinking of it, or it is in background. But when it comes to dance, dancer's body is in foreground. It is always available to her and is in "the moment". It is in this sense a dancer's body is always "present" to her. As a dancer there is a heightened awareness in and for the body. When a daily chore is executed it is not necessary that all the body is "present" to us, few parts of the body might be "absent" to us.

Sauṣṭhava and the present body are the two parameters, which are prerequisite for any form of dance. Thus having differentiated between non-dance and dance movement, we can say that dance movement is not just an external body movement but internal too. If thoughts are to be put in front of the world, then it needs body which utilizes space and understanding of the body and mind through *sauṣṭhava.*

To facilitate this understanding let us make a model of body, *manas* and *bhāva.*

Model of Body

We are making an attempt to make a model of body with seventeen joints. Let us begin with spinal cord with three joints. Rest of the body joints are knee, elbow, ankle, etc., we measure the angle made by each joint. To begin with, this model is evolved on the basis of Bharatanāṭyam dance but the quest does not stop there. A universal model applicable to dance forms across the globe can be evolved. The problem being faced is in visualizing the movement of spinal cord. Right now the so-called sliding movement of a torso, done in Oḍisī, a dance technique from Orissa (Odisha), eastern India, is more spring like, where the point in the middle of the spinal cord moves to the right and there is a feeling of torso bending to the left. Same way if eighth point of the spinal cord moves to left, there is a feeling of torso bending to the right. We still facing the problem of visualizing the spinal cord in joint, what I can see is a spring, which

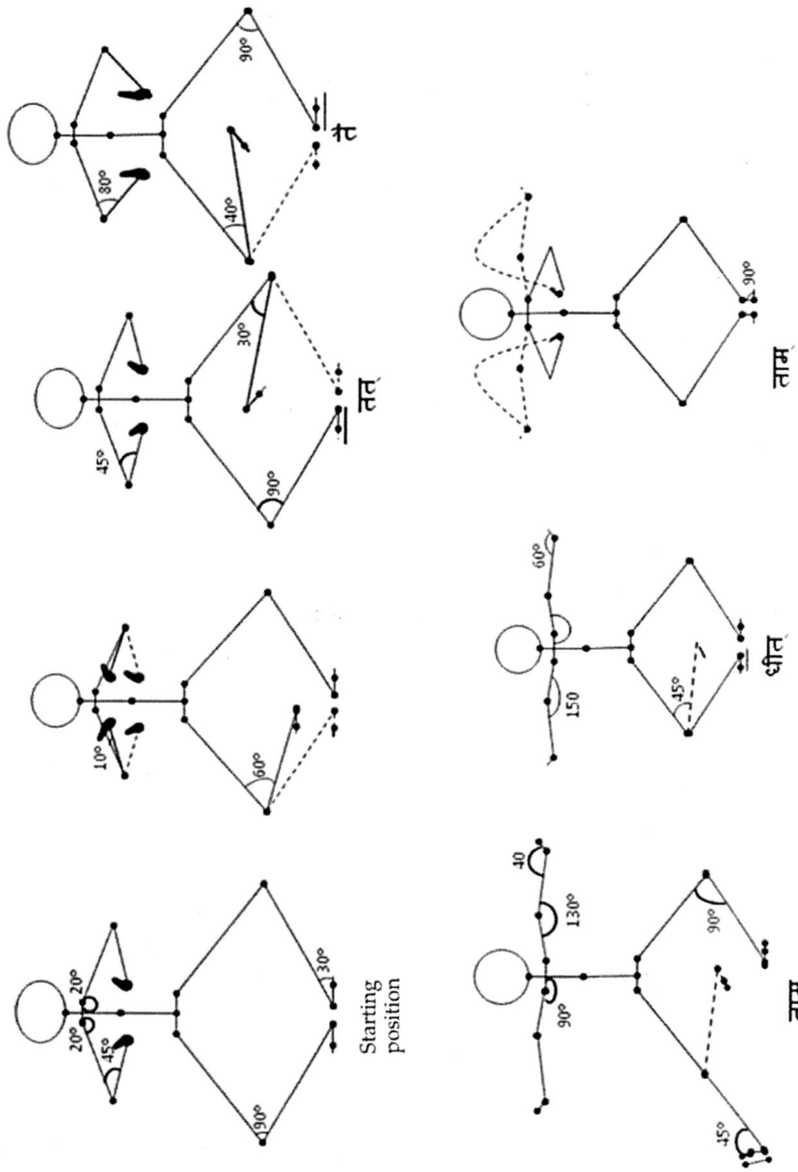

fig. 1: Movement sequence of pakkam adavu in Bharatanāṭyam style

can be bent or rotated as one would want. The only thing is that it does not bounce back as the spring would come, when left loose after giving pressure.

All the motion that takes place in the body is with the help of contraction and expansion of the muscles. This affects the joints and motion in joints. So we reduced all the motion of muscles in motion of joints as that is what is seen. Thus taking the model of a body with seventeen joints we look at a movement, and understand the degree of freedom in each joint. A movement sequence of an *adavu* from Bharatanāṭyam style is given in *fig*. 1.

In the second step of this *adavu*, hand is shown to go up from the elbow and from 10°, i.e. from 45° to 10°, the change is of almost 35°, but just to emphasis the movement, so as it is not missed, it is shown to be 10° whereas the change is of 10° only, i.e. from 45° to 35°. As you jump elbows also go with the movement hence the change is 10°. It is not possible to jump only with your feet and ignore or keep the upper body (above waist) static. One jumps with the whole body, though legs play a major role; so each and every joint is involved, hence the change.

Model of Manas

Manas is atomic in nature, it does not have any extension in space. It is the internal sense of the body. It moves in the internal body. *Manas* is the connecting link between *śarīra* and *ātman*. It carries the messages given by *ātman* to *śarīra* and *śarīra*'s (senses) message to *ātman*. Attention is the property of *manas*, that is why, even if all the senses are taking information from outside world at a time, we percieve one at a time because *manas* is at one place at a time. For example, while reading a book, attention is focused on the book so if someone calls the reader or an ant crawls over it, that is not perceived. That means to acquire knowledge it is important that *manas* is involved in that activity. Now *manas* cannot be at a time in all the five senses. At one point of time it is in one activity or sense.

So taking this viewpoint we trace the movement of *manas*. We chart out a model in which details of movement of *manas* are traced in a particular activity. Say, walking, how does *manas* move while walking?

At one point it is in one activity or sense. So taking this viewpoint, movement of *manas* is traced. A model is charted out in which details of movement of *manas* are traced in a particular activity. Say, walking. When we walk, how does *manas* move?

Fig. 2 shows the movement of *manas* of the *pakkam adavu* shown in *fig*. 1. Movement starts from the navel region, shown in gray colour and goes to pelvis and ends at point 52, which is the position of the hands.

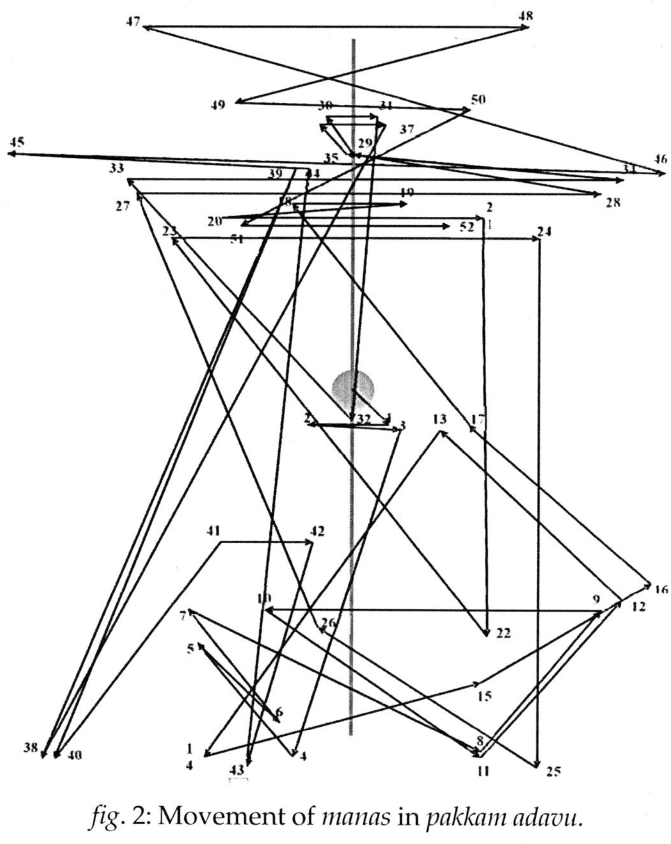

fig. 2: Movement of *manas* in *pakkam adavu*.

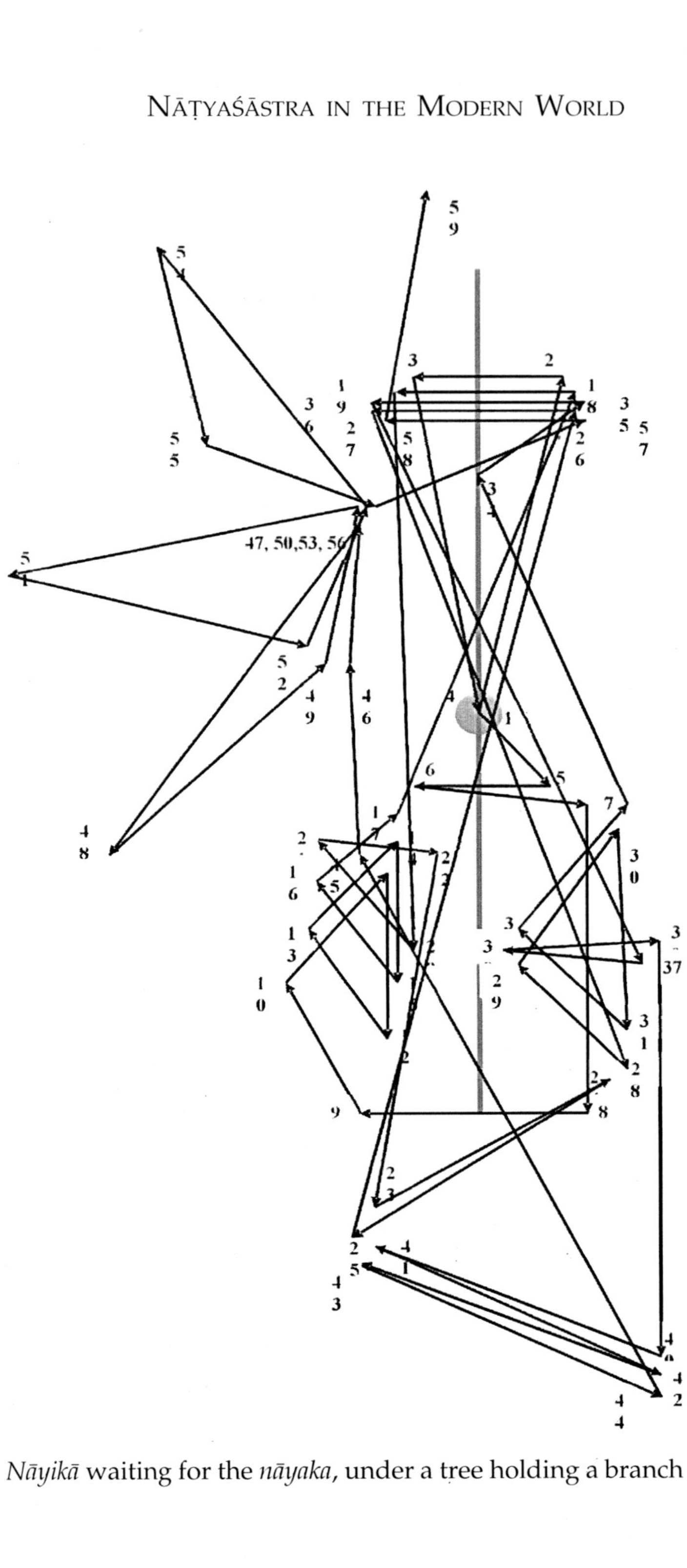

fig. 3: *Nāyikā* waiting for the *nāyaka*, under a tree holding a branch of a tree

Model of Bhāva

Using the same technique of *manas* given above, the motion of *bhāva* (emotions) is traced. As seen earlier, *bhāva*s are the postures of mind/ thought. When a particular *bhāva* rests in mind it transports action into body. It is a state of being.

We trace the motion of *bhāva*, as it was done for the model of body. The *nāyikā* is waiting. Here in *fig.* 3 we show a *nāyikā* waiting for her *nāyaka*, under a tree, holding a branch of a tree. Movement starts from the navel region, shown in gray colour and goes to pelvis and ends at point 59, which is the position of the hands.

Thus the above means of tracing the motion of *manas*, with the help of pause and motion will help to formulate *karaṇa*s, and apply it to *nṛtta*, *nṛtya* and *nāṭya*. The tier-C model will also be worked out later in future.

References

Asokamalla, Nṛtyādhyāya, tr. *Vachaspati Gairola in Hindi*, 1985, Delhi: Chowkhamba Publications.

Bose, Mandakranta, 2007, *Movement and Mimesis: The Idea of Dance in the Sanskrit Tradition*, New Delhi: D.K. Printworld.

Dhanañjaya, 2000, *Daśarūpaka* with commentery by Nandi, Upadhyaya Ramji, Bharatiya Vidya Sansthan.

Dhanañjaya, 2004, *Daśarūpaka*, Musalgaokar Kesharao, Varanasi: Chowkhamba Sanskrit Bhavan.

Fraleigh, Sondra, *Dance and the Lived Body*, Pennsylvania: University of Pittsburgh Press.

Johnstone, Maxine Sheets, 1999, *The Primacy of Movement*, Philadelphia: John Benjamins Publishing Company.

Johnstone, Maxine Sheets, ed., 1992, *Giving the Body Its Due*, Albany: State University of New York Press.

Johnstone, Maxine Sheets, ed., *Illuminating Dance: Philosophical Explorations*, Philadelphia: Bucknell University Press.

Johnstone, Maxine Sheets, 1963, *Phenomenology of Dance*, Madison: University of Wisconsin Press.

Leder, Drew, 1990, *The Absent Body*, Chicago: University of Chicago Press.

Mātrālakṣaṇam, ed. Kapila Vatsyayan, Delhi: Indira Gandhi National Centre for the Arts.

Nāṭyaśāstra of Bharatamuni, tr. Manmohan Ghosh, 2003, Varanasi: Chowkhamba Sanskrit Series.

Nāṭyaśāstra of Bharatamuni, 1996, with Abhinavagupta's commentary, with Hindi commentary by Dwivedi Parasnath, Varanasi: Sampurnanda Sankrit Viswavidyalaya.

Nāṭyaśāstra of Bharat Muni, 1981, with Abhinavagupta's, Abhinavabhāratī, ed. Madhusudan Shastri, Varanasi: Banaras Hindu University.

Thirumal, Swathi, 2004, *Bālarāmabharataṁ*, tr. Dr V.S. Varma, Trivandrum: V.S. Varma.

Vezina, Daneille, 2006, *Phenomenology of Dance*, Simon Fraser University, Canada.

Viṣṇudharmottara Purāṇa, tr. Priyabala Shah, 2002, Delhi: Parimal Publicaitons.

Zarrilli, Phillip, *When Body Becomes All Eyes*, New Delhi: Oxford University Press.

9

Nāṭyaśāstra and Its Regional Manifestations

Radhavallabh Tripathi

Nāṭyaśāstra (*NŚ*) was compiled to set models and standards for the playwrights and performers. Being *ākaragrantha* (sourcebook) as well as the most voluminous authentic ancient text on the art of drama, it naturally cast an everlasting impact on Indian theatric traditions including the regional traditions of performance. The philosophy and vision for theatre spelled out by *Nāṭyaśāstra* have percolated so deeply in forms of dance and drama in India that despite all the geographical, social and anthropological differences, this single unique text of Bharatamuni has paved the way for the sustenance of and synchronization between diverse regional theatric traditions of India. The tenets of *Nāṭyaśāstra* in some way or other are reflected in the regional theatre forms like:

- **North** : *Bhāṇḍa Pather* and *Bhāṇḍa* of Kashmir
- **North-East** : *Aṅkīya Naṭa, Lai Haroaba, Bare Chaharia Bhaona* (all from Assam), Manipuri *rāsa*, etc.
- **Northern India** : *Rāmalīlā, Rāsalālā, Svāṅga, Nauṭaṅkī,* etc.
- **Central India** : *Māñca* (in Malwa), *Nācā* (in Chhattisgarh)
- **Rajasthan** : *Khayāl*
- **Gujarat** : *Bhavāi*
- **Andhra Pradesh and Karnataka** : *Harikathā, Yakṣagāna, Kucipuḍī,* etc.

- **Kerala and Tamil Nadu** : *Kr̥ṣṇāṭṭam, Rāmāṭṭam, Therukūttu, Kathakali, Vīthīnāṭakam, Kūṭiyāṭṭam, Bhāgavatamelā*, etc.

There are certain features that all regional theatres share with each other, and these characteristics have been by and large borrowed by these regional theatres directly or indirectly from *Nāṭyaśāstra*. These features are: (i) The preliminaries or *pūrvaraṅga*; (ii) *rasa*-oriented aesthetics; (iii) non-linear concept of time and space; and (iv) philosophy and techniques of *abhinaya*, specially the *āṅgika abhinaya* (physical gesticulation) including the *karaṇa*s and the *aṅgahāra*s. Besides, a number of theatrical conventions like *kakṣyā-vibhāga* (division of the stage in imaginary zones) and *bhūmikā-vikalpa* (distribution of roles) required for visualizing such concepts were reflected in diverse regional traditions of performance through Bharata's vision of theatre.

Interaction between Veda and *loka*, *mārga* and *deśī*, and classic and folk has been a mark of Indian tradition. *Nāṭyaśāstra* defines *loka* (society) as one of the three *pramāṇa*s (parameters) for *nāṭya*, the other two being Veda (the Nāṭyaveda or Śāstra) and *adhyātma* (listening to the inner voice — actor's own discretion). Bharatamuni himself created a scope for an approach to the regional practices and regional forms for the performers by the way of recommending that if an actor cannot decide his course of action for the performance either through Śāstra or through his own discretion, he should approach *loka*. This apart, some of the fundamental elements of theatre that have been enumerated by him (VI.10), are also indirectly linked to regional practices. They are *lokadharmī* (the natural mode, under *dharmī* — the *modus operandi*), *vr̥tti*s (styles), *pravr̥tti*s (tendencies) and *mānuṣī siddhi* (human success) under *siddhi* (success). *Lokadharmī* is the practice of theatre in conformity to the behaviour of people in actual life. It hardly has any connection with folk theatre as sometimes it is supposed to have, neither does it mean adaptation of the practices of regional theatres. However, the terms used by Bharata to define *lokadharmī* imbibe a consideration for regional forms of theatre.

Lokadharmī is said to be the form of theatre that is enjoined with *lokavārtā-kriyā* (activities belonging to life of people at empirical level) and devoid of any playful display of various parts of the body of the performer, devoid of any decor that is added out of imagination by the performer. It is true that most of traditional forms of theatre as prevailing in different regions adopt the *nāṭyadharmī* (conventional mode) in a greater degree that the *lokadharmī*, but the very inclusive nature of the latter as spelled out by Bharata has scope for introducing regional theatric practices.

The concept of *pravṛtti* is very much linked to the theory of *lokadharmī*. *Pravṛtti* means studying the actual tendencies of human behaviour as prevailing in different regions. To illustrate *pravṛtti*s, Bharata divides the Indian subcontinent into four regions, and on the basis of this division four types of *pravṛtti*s are defined. An actor is supposed to study the behavioural patterns of diverse regions of this country as well as regional theatre practices.

Bharata was aware of diverse regional theatre practices represented by the minor forms of drama which were later on termed as *uparūpaka*s. In the last chapter of *Nāṭyaśāstra*, he informs that his sons, trained by him in Nāṭyaveda later on began to perform the *śilpaka*s of rustic nature (*grāmyadharmaka*). *Śilpaka* is one of the *uparūpaka*s. The sons of Bharata, in the *śilpaka*s performed by them, presented the life and deeds of the sages residing in the vicinity of Himalayas by the way of *viḍambana* (caricature) and *vyaṅgyakaraṇa* (satire). The sages being laughed at in this way, got infuriated and cursed the actors to be expelled from the divine region of the Himalayas and to become śūdras. Ultimately, Bharatamuni asked them to go towards south and continue with their performances.

This episode from the *Nāṭyaśāstra* suggests that Bharata was sympathetic to those who experimented with regional forms of theatre. He has been not only studying these forms closely, he also adopted the motifs and techniques from the regional forms of theatre in formulating his system of classical theatre. The very concept of *prayoga* or the types of the theatric performance confirms the tendency in *Nāṭyaśāstra* for allowances to regional forms. *Prayoga* is mainly of two types — *ābhyantara* (internal) and *bāhya* (external). The *ābhyantara prayoga* is performed by trained artists and stands in total commitment to Śāstra. The performers of *bāhya prayoga* on the other hand, might be completely ignorant of the Śāstra, or might have studied Śāstra with the masters (*nāṭyācāryas*), but guided by their own intuition or skill, they can transgress the norms of the Śāstra or take liberty with its dicta due to their contact with the regional theatre forms. Bharata says that such actors should be allowed to go on with their performances (that might be following regional variations) (XXII.77-80). The *bāhya prayoga* is thus a theatre of the people. *Nāṭyaśāstra* in this way makes room for the inclusion of regional forms and local colours in its classical mould.

Siddhi is of two types — *daivī* (divine) and *mānuṣī* (human). In the former, the audience transcend their own time–space frame to reach a different level of time and space. They are in complete harmony with the sentiments projected through the performance and quite attuned to the world created there. With a perfect sense of belonging to this another level of time and space, they are not even in a position to react to the performance as an art. The trio of the actor, audience and the poetic world is merged in a harmony. In *mānuṣī siddhi,* however, the situation is quite different. The contents of the play in performance are communicated by the actor to the spectator through an interpretative method. The actor and the spectator both are aware of the process of communication and the method of interpretation that the performer employs. The later visualizes the performance remaining rooted in his own frame of time and space and is able to appreciate the performance unfolding a different level of time and space. The actor stands as an interpreter between this level and the historic present of the spectator. He is a medium leading them to the vision of the world as conceived by the dramatist or the poet. The spectator can perceive this world and at the same time he can also appreciate the quality of the performance by the actor. He remains in the state of flux — between involvement and detachment. The state of awareness is maintained throughout. The application of the *mānuṣī siddhi* would bring theatre close to the regional theatric practices. The *sūtradhāra* addresses the audience in many regional theatre forms to create an "alienation effect". The audience can enjoy the play in performance and appreciate it in various ways, they can even exhibit their appreciation for an actor by immediately showering gifts, etc. on him or her (XXVII.2-13).

In his discourse on *bhūmikā-vikalpa* (ascribing roles), Bharata has classified the *bhūmikā* (assumption of roles) by the actors in three types — *anurūpā* (congruous), *virūpā* (incongruous) and *rūpānusāriṇī* (tending to become similar), depending on the aptitude of the performer, i.e. whether he or she is alike to the role, he or she is unlike to it, or he or she tends to become alike with it. Bharata would prefer the *anurūpā* type only, but at the same time, he allows the other two types also, depending on the circumstances. This brings out the multiplicity of theatric traditions that have influenced the *Nāṭyaśāstra*. Many regional forms of theatre, take recourse to *virūpā* and *rūpānusāriṇī* types of *bhūmikā*s, i.e. female characters being enacted by the male actors, the role of a young man being done by an actor quite old in age, etc.

Nāṭyāyita is one of the six types of *śārīra abhinaya* under *sāmānya abhinaya* as described in *Nāṭyaśāstra* (chap. XXII). In *nāṭyāyita* an actor performing a character joins the song being sung about that very particular character, which he or she is rendering. Alternately, the actors form an audience to watch the play within the play on the stage. Bharata also discusses the concept of *līlā* in his treatment of *sāmānya abhinaya*. *Līlā* evinces the typical practice prevailing in various forms of folk theatres and the element of alienation in the performance. In *līlā* the heroine narrates or performs the character or deeds of her lover before her friends. She thus distances herself from her own role to assume another role. The performance of *śrīgadita*, a precursor to *līlā* theatre, is characterized by *līlā*.

Bharata has not dealt with any one of these minor forms of drama — or the regional forms of theatre, except *nāṭikā*, and *nāṭikā* in no way can be adjusted or identified as any regional form of theatre, it is created by blending and shortening of *nāṭaka* and *prakaraṇa* for the purpose of performance in a royal court.

Nāṭyaśāstra is a text on the *mārga* (classic) tradition of our theatre and its author left the exposition of the *deśī* (regional traditions) to his successors. He proclaims at the end of *Nāṭyaśāstra* that whatever has been left out by me will be taken up by Kohala in his *Uttaratantra* (XXXVII.18). In the first chaper of *Nāṭyaśāstra*, Kohala's name is mentioned in the list of 100 disciples of Bharata that were present when Bharata delivered his discourse on *Nāṭyaśāstra* before Ātreya and other sages in reply to their five queries. Mahendra Sūri, Hemacandra's student, has referred to Kohala as a *muni* (sage) and one of the disciples of Bharatamuni. From references by Abhinavagupta, Hemacandra, Rāmacandra-Guṇacandra Sāgaranandin and a host of other authors, we gather that Kohala did compose his own *Nāṭyaśāstra*, but this work — sometimes referred as *Kohalīyanāṭyaśāstra*, is no more extant. There are a number of later texts on *nāṭya* (theatre), *nṛtya* (dance) or *saṅgīta* (music) dealing with regional theatre forms. The text of Kohala was available to the authors of some of these texts, and also most probably to Abhinavagupta, Rāmacandra-Guṇacandra and Hemacandra.

Nṛttaratnāvalī (*NR*) of Jāyasenāpati is one of the most comprehensive texts on dance, and it provides most extensive treatment of the subject with definitions of regional varieties of various categories — *deśīnṛtta, deśīpāda, deśīcārī*s, *deśīkaraṇa*s, etc. In fact, *Nṛttaratnāvalī* and Someśvara's stupendous work on arts — *Mānasollāsa* or *Abhilāṣitārthacintāmaṇi* — are two of the most authentic texts providing extensive treatment on the regional theatre forms. At the very outset of *Mānasollāsa* Someśvara says that he was enamoured seeing the folk dances of the community of śabaras (a tribe) and he wanted to adopt such dances for the presentations in his court.

Deśī as been defined as the gamut of variations resulting due to regional practices in dance, drama and music. Śārṅgadeva in his *Saṅgītaratnākara* (*SR*) defines *deśī* as the way of performance prevalent in diverse regions (*SR*, I.23). Śāradātanaya in his *Bhāvaprakāśa* (*BP*) says that *deśī* is a musical composition in regional language (*BP*, chap. 10, p. 390). Sudhākalaśa, in his *Saṅgītasāroddhāra* (I.8) rightly expands the idea of *deśī* to *gīta* (songs), *vādya* (percussions) and *nāṭya*. *Nāṭyasarvasvadīpikā* (*NSD*) attributed to Ādibharata describes the special feature of *deśī* traditions of dance, songs and music in respect of their quality of appeasement to local masses and their receptivity for change according to popular taste (*NSD*, II.2.26). Śārṅgadeva in *Saṅgītaratnākara* and Mataṅga in *Bṛhaddeśī* provide extensive treatment to *deśī* traditions of music and dance. A text *Deśīnṛttasaṁudra* has been referred by V. Raghavan that is no longer available.

Other texts that refer to or provide definitions of minor or regional forms of drama are *Nāṭyadarpaṇa* (*ND*) of Rāmacandra and Guṇacandra, Bhoja's *Śṛṅgāraprakāśa* (*ŚP*), Hemacandra's *Kāvyānuśāsana* (*KS*), Sāgaranandin's *Nāṭakalakṣaṇaratnakośa* (*NLRK*), Amṛtānandayogin's *Alaṁkārasaṁgraha* (*AS*), Vipradāsa's *Saṅgītacandra* (*SC*), *Sāhityadarpaṇa* (*SD*) of Viśvanātha, Puṇḍarīka Viṭṭhala's *Nartananirṇaya* (*NN*), Kumbhakarṇa's *Nṛttaratnakośa* and *Saṅgītarāja* (*SR*), Śubhaṅkara's *Saṅgītadāmodara* (*SaṅD*), Raghunātha's *Nāṭyamanoramā* (*NM*) and *Nṛttasaṁgraha* (*NṛS*) by an anonymous author.

As we are not in possession of the text of Kohala or *Kohalīyanāṭyaśāstra*, it is not possible to say what term he had used to denote the regional forms of theatre. Abhinavagupta seems to have gone through the text of Kohala and he very often cites or refers to Kohala. *Nṛttaprabandha* — the term used by Abhinavagupta for regional theatric forms or minor forms of drama may have been borrowed from Kohala. Abhinavagupta quotes the definitions of some of the *nṛttaprabandha*s attributing them to *cirantana*s (the ancients or some ancient master). In all probability, these definitions are from the text of Kohala that is now lost to us.

As the regional forms have been constantly growing, and were constantly being defined and redefined by the *ācārya*s in Bharata's tradition, several optional terms are used for these so-called *nṛttaprabandha*s. *Nṛtya*, *saṁkīrṇa rūpaka* and *anya rūpaka* are the terms that can be applied to these minor forms of drama according to Dhanañjaya and Dhanika (*Daśarūpaka*, *vṛtti* on I.8, III.33); Hemacandra uses the term *geyarūpaka* for them; Śubhaṅkara, Dattila and Sāgaranandin call them *gauṇarūpaka*s (minor plays), while authors of *Nāṭyadarpaṇa* use the term *anya rūpaka* (other plays) for them. It is in *Alaṁkārasaṁgraha* and *Sāhityadarpaṇa* that these forms of drama find the nomenclature of the *uparūpaka*. They are also called *deśī rūpaka*s or *deśya prabandha*s. In fact, they are prototypes of a variety of regional forms of theatre in this vast peninsula.

There can be no limit to the number of these *deśī* forms of drama. Considering the multiplicity of traditions that these minor forms belong to, we find that the number is constantly increasing, and contrary to the limit of ten that is mostly accepted in case of the number of *rūpaka*s, any attempt to prescribe a limit of number for these regional forms could be futile. We find that the *ācārya*s had been observing the process of emergence of new forms of theatre in different regions and their growth in relation to regional variations and they were also trying to define and standardize the emerging new forms.

Abhinavagupta has quoted the definitions of the following regional forms of theatre named as *nṛttaprabandha*s, as given by some ancient *ācārya* or *ācāryas* — *rāsaka*, *ḍombī*, *prasthāna*, *bhāṇikā*, *bhāṇa*, *ṣidgaka*, *hallīsaka* and *rāmākrīḍa*. Elsewhere, he has given a detailed description of *ḍombikā* or *ḍombī*. Dhanika has enumerated *ḍombī, śrīgadita, bhāṇa, bhāṇī, prasthāna, rāsaka* and *kāvya* as seven varieties of *nṛtya* like *bhāṇa* (*bhāṇa* here is different from the *rūpaka* named *bhāṇa*). Amṛtānandayogin in his *Alaṁkārasaṁgraha* (IX.2-3) has defined sixteen *uparūpakas* — *nāṭikā, saṭṭaka, troṭaka, goṣṭhī, prekṣaṇaka, bhāṇikā, saṁllāpaka, prasthāna, kāvya, hallīsa, rāsaka, śrīgadita, lāsikā, durmallī, nāṭyarāsaka* and *ullāpya*. Viśvanātha adds *prakaraṇī* and *śilpaka*, in this list, and makes them eighteen (*SD* VI.5). Viśvanātha and some other authors talk of eighteen *uparūpakas*, which are — *nāṭikā, troṭaka, goṣṭhī, saṭṭaka, nāṭyarāsaka, prasthāna, ullāpyaka, kāvya, citrakāvya, preṅkhaṇa, rāsaka, saṁlāpaka, śrīgadita, śilpaka, vilāsikā, durmallikā, prakaraṇī, hallīsa* and *bhāṇikā*. *Agni Purāṇa* and *Śṛṅgāraparakāśa* count twenty-seven and twenty-four types of *rūpakas* and they include the regional forms also in their treatment. Śāradātanaya raises the number to thirty by adding *mallikā, kalpavallī* and *pārijātaka* (*BP*, chap. VIII, p. 221). Out of the thirty *rūpakas* that he has cited, ten are *rasātmaka* and remaining twenty are *bhāvātmaka* according to him.

It is Jāyasenāpati who introduces a number of local forms of dance-drama and even dances belonging to the tribes and rural areas in south in this gamut of *uparūpakas* or *nṛttaprabandhas*, such as — *daṇḍarāsaka, carcarīnāṭyam śabaranṛtyam kaivāra, gharghara, vāgaḍanṛttam preraṇīpaddhati, śivapriyanṛttam, cintunṛttam, kandukanṛttam, bhāṇḍikanṛttam, cāraṇanṛttam, dohakanṛttam, bahurūpanṛttam* and *kollāṭanṛttam*.

Nāṭyamanoramā and *Nṛttasaṁgraha* define *jakkaḍī* — a dance form accompanied with songs in mlechcha *bhāṣā* or Persian languages. It is performed by the Yavanas. *Kavikāmadhenu*, a text quoted in *Bharatakośa* by Ramakrishna Kavi, deals with a form of drama called *deśya* (*BK* 283). It is composed in a regional language, has three *sandhis*, and consists of descriptions of spring festivals and beauties of this earth. It also presents descriptions of war, the rogues as characters and has either *śṛṅgāra* or *vīra* as dominant *rasas*.

The number of these so-called *uparūpaka*s went on increasing from one (in Bharata's *Nāṭyaśāstra*) to more than forty. Many of these are dance-dramas prevailing in different regions. Some of them are mere songs or dances, they are included in the gamut of these regional theatre forms as combined with narration of an episode or presentation of a theme, they also assumed dramatic proportions.

Considering the nomenclatures and characteristics of these *nṛttaprabandha*s, *nṛtya*s, *deśīrūpaka*s, *geyarūpaka*s or *uparūpaka*s, we can identify many of them as regional forms of theatre that are still being practised today in some part or the other of this vast peninsula. For example, *prekṣaṇaka* is defined by the authors of *Śṛṅgāraprakāśa* and *Nāṭyadarpaṇa* as a play that has many special characters and is performed in the streets, *samāja*s (social gatherings or fares) and pubs, etc. (*SP* XI.311; *ND* IV.218). *Prekṣaṇaka* has been a folk form confined to the Madhyadeśa (central part of the country) and Gujarat. The southern regions had different traditions of *prekṣaṇaka*, as *Bhāvaprakāśa* and *Alaṁkārasaṁgraha* (IX.122-25) define it as a play full of robust actions and involving characters of low status (*hīnanāyaka*) to be performed without a *sūtradhāra* (stage manager). *Nartanaka* seems to be a graceful form of *prekṣaṇaka* and is characterized by *padārthābhinaya* (*BP*, chap. IX, p. 263), *saṭṭaka* can be taken to be regional variation of *nāṭikā*. If we take into account the geographical area in which most of the *saṭṭaka*s were composed and performed, it is Madhyadeśa. In the same way, a *nāṭaka* becomes *toṭaka* or *troṭaka* when dances and songs in local languages are introduced within its texture *Vikramorvaśīyam* of Kālidāsa, the sole available specimen of *toṭaka* or *troṭaka* has become a unique specimen of folk forms or regional forms of ancient Indian theatre.

Ḍombī is feminine of *ḍomba*, *ḍombikā* is its synonym. Like *śrīgadita*, it belongs to the theatre of females. *Ḍomba* was a tribe in ancient India. The word *ḍoma* derived from it is used in languages of north India for sweepers and scavengers. The female dancer performing *ḍombī* is also called *ḍombī* or *ḍombikā*. *Ḍombī* was a form abounding in songs, music and dances. The songs accompanying its performance were also called *ḍombī*-songs and the accompanying dance was also called *ḍombī* dance (*Abh.*, pt. I, p. 181). Abhainavagupta suggests that the dancer called *ḍombī* sings the *gāthās* and also performs on them. This singing and performance is accompanied with her narration. This feature of narration in accompaniment to dance and singing is a precursor of *Harikathā* as practised in Andhra and Karnataka, and also brings *ḍombī* very close to the minor forms like *bhāṇa* and *bhāṇikā*, so that the later theorists have even confused between *ḍombī*, *bhāṇa* and *bhāṇikā*. From the description of *ḍombikā* or *ḍombī*, provided by Abhinavagupta and Kalhaṇa, it is also clear that it was a regional form of theatre practised in the locality of Kashmir. Hemacandra thinks that it might have originated from the *deśī nṛtya*. Abhinavagupta says that *ḍombī* is full of grace and *rasa* and the poets have been composing new *ḍombīs* in *jātibhāṣā* (local dialects) (*Abh.*, pt. IV, p. 280).

Goṣṭhī, *rāsaka*, *daṇḍarāsaka*, *nāṭyarāsaka* and *hallīsaka* — all these forms are dances or dance-dramas that have been in vogue in agrarian society. They basically belonged to Kṛṣṇa-cult and introduction of secular themes in their performances might have occurred at a later stage. The definitions of *goṣṭhī* given in *Bhāvaprakāśa* and *Sāhityadarpaṇa* establish it as a proto-type of *rāsalīlā*. Basically, it must have been a small play or dance representing the deeds of Kṛṣṇa performed by the *gopa* community (shepherds) in the vicinity of a *goṣṭha* (pan) (*SP* 11.308). *Bhāvaprakāśa*, however, allows the possibility of other themes also for *goṣṭhī* by the way of prescribing the plot of *goṣṭhī* as *utpādya* (imaginary) (*BP*, chap. VIII, p. 256).

Rāsaka is a circular dance involving various items in *latā*, *bhedyaka*, *piṇḍī*, etc. by as many as sixty-four performers (*Abh.* in *NŚ* chap. IV). On the other hand, *Alaṁkārasaṁgraha* (IX.138-51), *Saṅgītadāmodara* (p. 95), *Nāṭakalakṣaṇaratnakośa* (p. 304) and *Sāhityadarpaṇa* (VI.290) define *rāsaka* as a farce with a fool as a hero, given to rustic ways. *Saṅgītadāmodara* retains both alternatives —

rāsaka as a play depicting the deeds of the boy Kṛṣṇa and *rāsaka* as a secular farce. In *nāṭyarāsaka*, some female characters re-enact the acts of Lord Kṛṣṇa. It is a play full of love and romance, set in the mood of spring season. Later *ācārya*s however give an alternate set of definitions identifying *nāṭyarāsaka* as a play with a great hero and a *pīṭhamarda* as his assistant, and a lady in love waiting for the hero (*BP*, chap. IX, p. 263; *SD* VI.285; *AS* IX.159-61). *Rāsaka* and *nāṭyarāsaka* assume the form of *daṇḍarāsaka* if the dancers are holding sticks for beating and they become *hallīsaka* if the dance movements are circular (*SP* XI.309). *Bhāvaprakāśa* (chap. IX, pp. 266-67), *Alaṁkārasaṁgraha* (IX.136-38) and *Sāhityadarpaṇa* (VI.298) define *hallīsaka* as a play with secular themes. *Hallīsaka* has close resemblance with *carcarī* and *chalita* also (Vema, *BK*, p. 203).

As per definitions given in *Śṛṅgāraprakāśa* (XI.280-81), *Bhāvaprakāśa* (chap. IX, p. 258), *Sāhityadarpaṇa* (VI.292-93) and *Alaṁkārasaṁgraha* (chap. IX, 51b-153a), *śrīgadita* is similar to *nāṭyarāsaka* in respect of its theme. *Śidgaka* is a counterpart of *nāṭyarāsaka* or *śrīgadita*. A representation of the mischief of the husband by a lady becomes *śidgaka* (*Abh*, chap. IV). *Prasthāna* is a dance or a dance-drama based on the theme of departure. In the definition as quoted by Abhinavagupta, it is a graceful form where the dance movements are based on the march of elephants and other animals. Other *ācārya*s define it as a play with amorous sentiments and based on delineating the theme of separation. *Alaṁkārasaṁgraha* prescribes that characters of low community — the *dāsa*s and *dāsī*s as its protagonists, and depiction of scenes of drinking, etc. as its theme. *Śṛṅgāraprakāśa* visualizes the use of four *apasārakas* (songs) in it (*Abh.*, chap. IV; *SP* XI.283-85; *BP* chap. IX, p. 262; *AS* IX.131-33; *SD* VI.286). *Ullopyaka* and *śilpaka* are closely related. The twenty-seven components of *śilpaka* are used in *ullopyaka*, it has tableau of gods or heroes profusely adorned with bright costumes (*BP*, chap. IX, p. 266; *AS* IX.161-62; *SD* VI.287). *Sallāpaka* (*saṁlāpaka* or *sallāpa*) resembles the *rūpaka*s like *samavakāra* and *ḍima*, depicting scenes like attack and surrounding a city (*SD* VI.291; *BP*, chap. VIII, p. 256; *AS* IX.133b-136a, IX.136b-131a). *Mattallikā*, *mallikā*, *pārijātakam* / *pārijātalatā* and *kalpavallī* these forms are based on narration and singing of *gāthās*. *Preṅkhaṇam*, *durmallikā* / *durmilitā* / *durmallī* and *śilpakam*-type of plays present people of low caste and characters of lower strata of society, or *viṭas*, *pīṭhamardas*, etc. (*SD* VI.289, VI.293; *ND*, p. 191; *SP* XI.282-83; *BP*, chap. IX, p. 267, chap. VIII, p. 257; *AS* IX.155-58). *Vilāsikā* or *lāsikā* is described only in two texts — *Alaṁkārasaṁgraha* and *Sāhityadarpaṇa*.

From the foregoing account of *uparūpakas*, it is clear that they are closely related to regional theatre forms. Sometimes the *ācāryas* like Bhoja, Someśvara and others define an *uparūpaka* itself as a regional form of theatre. Some of the *uparūpakas* can be identified with particular regional theatre forms that are still in practice with slight variations, for example, *nāṭyarāsaka* and *daṇḍarāsaka* have manifested as the *garabā* in Gujarat, and the *rāsaka* and *hallīsaka* have become *rāsalīlā* in northern parts of the country as well as *bhāgavatamelā* or *vīthīnāṭakam* in southern parts. *Ḍombī*, *bhāṇa*, *bhāṇī* or *bhāṇikā* have evolved in various forms like Paṇḍavānī in central parts of the country; *harikathā* or *kīrtaniyanāṭa* in north-east and southern regions.

The interaction between the performance traditions of the *rūpakas* and the *uparūpakas* paved the way for emergence of regional theatre forms. Some of the *uparūpakas* or regional forms that were basically community dances or folk dances got enriched by drawing elements from the performance traditions of the *rūpakas* and the *uparūpakas* and assumed larger dramatic proportions. The enactment of particular themes or episodes in *uparūpakas* has shaped the regional theatre forms to a great extent. The performance of the animals in *prasthāna* led to enactment of *daśāvatāra* (Viṣṇu's ten incarnations) in many regional theatre forms.

It is the way of blending *lāsyāṅgas* that gives a local habitation to many forms of drama. *Lāsyāṅga*s are used in some of the major forms of drama (*daśarūpaka*s) also as per definitions in Bharata's text. They are employed in *vīthī* and *bhāṇa* (*rūpaka*). Some of the *lāsyāṅga*s assume the characteristics of regional theatres. For example, the tenth *lāsyāṅga* is *uktapratyukta*, consisting of interesting repartees and rejoinders in the dialogues. This *uktapratyukta* and *trimūḍhaka* together with *nāndī*, *prarocanā* and *bharatavākya* are used in some form or the other in various regional forms of theatres.

The narration by *sūtradhāra* is a feature that distinguishes the two performance traditions of *rūpaka*s and *uparūpakas*. *Sūtradhāra* has various names in different regional theatre forms. In Kūṭiyāṭṭam of Kerala, the *vidūṣaka* performs the functions of a *sūtradhāra*. *Sūtradhāra* in *terukūttu* or *vīthīnāṭakam* is called *kattiyakaran*, and he goes on addressing the audience and also having exchange of words with other characters. His interference on the stage when the drama is being performed is called *pottuvacanam*.

The authors in the field of Nāṭyaśāstra have always been re-adjusting various categories or enlarging them in view of the developments in the performance traditions. Sometimes such amendments come due to the impact of regional forms of theatre also, especially the multiplication in the number of *hasta*s, *sthānaka*s, etc. and the addition of *deśī* forms of *cārī*s, *hasta*s, *pāda*s, etc. must owe their origin to the regional forms of theatres. In fact, there is a growing tendency amongst the followers of Bharata to search the counterparts of various categories described by the great master in regional theatre forms.

Kerala has provided the most vibrant stage for correspondences with the *Nāṭyaśāstra*, and the dialogue between the classic and the regional traditions of theatre. The theatre of Kūṭiyāṭṭam thrived for centuries and continued to enthrall the audiences with its authentic exposition of Bharata's texts combined with improvizations. Kerala has also given us some of the most fascinating texts on actual performance of Sanskrit plays.

Contributors

Lyne Bansat-Boudon is *agrégée de grammaire*, Professor at the Section of Religious Sciences of the École pratique des hautes études (EPHE) in Paris where she holds the chair of "Indian Religions: Shaiva Studies". She is also an Honorary Senior Member of the Institut Universitaire de France. Her main fields of research are Sanskrit Drama and Indian Aesthetics as well as Non-dualist Kashmiri Shaivism. See in particular her D.Lit. thesis published as *Poétique du théatre indien*. She has also published *Lectures du Nāṭyaśāstra* (EFEO, 1992) and (in collaboration with Prof. K.D. Tripathi) *An Introduction to Tantric Philosophy: The Paramārthasāra of Abhinavagupta, with the Commentary of Yogarāja* (Routledge, 2011) [*address*: 53, Rue Manin, 75019 Paris (France), *e-mail*: <lyne.bansat-boudon@ephe.sorbonne.fr>].

Gajanana S. Hegde, MA, Ph.D., Diploma in Epigraphy, is a retired Associate Professor of Sanskrit, J.S.S. College, Dharwad, Karnataka. He is an amateur artist of *Yakṣagāna* and research scholar of south Indian dance–drama. He has written *Yakṣagāna Hasthabhinaya-darpana, Yakṣagāna and Its Sanskrit Sources, Concept of Dance in Classical Sanskrit Literature, A Peep into Sanskrit Dramaturgy and Yakṣagāna, Kūṭiyāṭṭam* and *Yakṣagāna: A Comparative Study*. He has completed three UGC research projects on Sanskrit Dramaturgy and south Indian dance–dramas. He has authored twenty research articles in English, thirty in Kannada and one play in Sanskrit. He has given four demo lectures on Sanskrit Dramaturgy, *Yakṣagāna*, and south Indian dance–dramas at Shilpakorn and Mahidol University of Bangkok; Kyoto University, Japan; and University of Bhutan, Bhutan [*address*: C/o # 28 Matrashree, Mahishi Road, Yemmikeri Malamaddi, Dharwad – 580 001 (Karnataka), *e-mail*: <gshy@ rediffmail.com>].

Natalia R. Lidova, Ph.D. in Sanskrit Studies, Senior Researcher, Department of Asian and African Literature, Institute of World Literature, Russian Academy of Sciences. Her main areas of research are Sanskrit Drama, Early Hindu Culture, Poetics, Ritual Studies and Modern Indian Theatre (*Kūṭiyāṭṭam*). Lidova has authored many articles and several books, including

Drama and Ritual of Early Hinduism (1994, 2nd edn. 1996), in which she substantiates a new hypothesis on the origin of ancient Indian theatre within the post-Vedic cult of *pūjā* [*address*: Institute of World Literature, Russian Academy of Sciences, Povarskaya 25A, Moscow 121069 (Russia), *e-mail*: <nlidova@gmail.com>].

Klara Gönc Moačanin, Working mostly on *Nāṭyaśāstra* and *Mahābhārata*. Teaching Indian literature (*Nāṭya*, *Śravya*, Neo-Indo-Āryan and Draviḍian Literature, Indian Art, Indian History, Asian Theatre, Sanskrit Seminars (on *Mahābhārata*, Kālidāsa, Bhāsa, Nāṭyaśāstra, Śūdraka, etc.). Interested in comparative literature – published a book (in Croatian) *Theatrical Practice of Classical Theatrical Forms: Greek Tragedy–Indian Nāṭya–Japanese* , and a number of articles in Croatian and English. Translated Śūdrakas's *Mṛcchakaṭika* for Croatian National Thetare that was performed in 1979-80. She has made translations from English, French, Hungarian and Sanskrit [*address*: Senior Lecturer, Department of Indology and Far Eastern Studies, Faculty of Philosophy, I. Lucica 3, 10000 Zagreb, Croatia, *e-mail*: <29wisteria@gmail.com>].

Sonal Nimbkar is a *Bharatnāṭyam* dancer. She is currently pursuing her Ph.D. from Centre for Exact Humanities at IIIT-H under the guidance of Prof. Navjyoti Singh and is also a lecturer in the same institute. Her research is to formulate the grammar of dance. She is tracing the smallest unit of movement which will be understood in the light of *karaṇa*s given in *Nāṭyaśāstra* [*address*: Centre for Exact Humanities (CEH), International Institute of Information Technology (IIIT-H), Gachibowli, Hyderabad – 500 032; *e-mail*: <sonal.nimkar@iiit.ac.in>].

Anvita Sharma, born in 1964, did her MA from Vikram University, Ujjain, in 1987. She did her research on *Nāṭyaśāstra* from the Dept. of Sanskrit, Banaras Hindu University and got her Ph.D. in 1992. Trained in *Bharatanāṭyam* style and having an access to German language, she carried forward her researches in the domain of *Nāṭyaśāstra* and brought out her work in Hindi entitled *Nāṭyaśāstra meiṅ Rasa evaṁ Bhāva*. The work comprises the editing of the text of 6th and 7th chapters of *Nāṭyaśāstra* with textual criticism and critical study of the theory of *rasa* and *bhāva*. Presently an Assistant Professor in Sahitya at Shri Lal Bahadur Shastri Rashtriya Vidyapeeth (Deemed University), New Delhi, she has been actively participating in national as well as international conferences and seminars on Nāṭyaśāstra, Sanskrit Literature and Contemporary Dimensions of the Sanskrit Literary Criticism. She is one of the emerging scholars of Nāṭyaśāstra [*address*: Sh Lal Bahadur Shastri

Rashtriya Sanskrit Vidyapeeth, Qutab Institutional Area, New Delhi, *e-mail*: <anvitasharma_01@yahoo.co.in>].

Navjyoti Singh is a philosopher and founder head of the Centre for Exact Humanities, at IIIT-H. His current research interest is in formal ontology, particularly ontology of society and ontology of arts. His basic work is in Jaina theory of transfinite numbers and Vaiśeṣika ontology. He has published about thirty research papers. His edited books include *Temporality and Logical Structure: An Indian Perspective* and *Srsti: Its Philosophical Entailments* [*address*: Centre for Exact Humanities (CEH), International Institute of Information Technology (IIIT-H), Gachibowli, Hyderabad – 500 032; *e-mail*: <navjyoti@iiit.ac.in>].

Kamalesh Datt Tripathi, Professor Emeritus, Department of Dharma-Āgama (Religious and Agamic Studies), Faculty of Sanskrit Learning and Theology, BHU, is an accomplished scholar of Indology. He is accredited with the starting of studies and research programmes in Āgamas at BHU. He worked also as the Director of Kālidāsa Akademi, Ujjain. Prof. Tripathi is a recipient of Certificate of Merit Award from the President of India in 2007 and number of other prestigious awards including Fellowship of Sangeet Natak Akademi. A widely-travelled scholar, he attended numerous International Conferences/Seminars. He was a visting professor to many foreign universities since 1996. Presently, he is Chief Editor and Director of Nāṭyaśāstra Project for bringing out an edition of Nepali Version of *Nāṭyaśāstra* preserved in the manuscripts of Nepal so far unutilized. [*address*: Plot no. 141/1, Susuwahi-Nasirpur Marg, Prajnapuram Colony, Near Nasirpur Aam ki Bagia, P.O. BHU, Varanasi - 221 005; *e-mail*: <igrkk_vns@dataone.in>].

Radhavallabh Tripathi has specialized in Nāṭyaśāstra and Sāhityaśāstra. His publications in these areas include *Nāṭyaśāstraviśvakośa* (an Encyclopaedic Dictionary of Nāṭyaśāstra), *Nāṭyalalitakalāsaṁgraha* (an Anthology of Texts on Performing and Plastic Arts), *Lectures on Nāṭyaśāstra*, *Aspects of Naṭyaśāstra*, *Bhāratīya Sāhityaśāstra ki Ācāryaparamparā* and *Nayā Sahityaśāstra* [*address*: M-83, II Floor, South City I, Gurgaon - 122 001 (Haryana) *e-mail*: <radhavallabh2002@gmail.com>].